CONFESSIONS
OF A
BRIEFLESS BARRISTER

CONFESSIONS
OF A
BRIEFLESS
BARRISTER

HARRY MITCHELL QC

Matador
9 Priory Business Park,
Wistow Road, Kibworth Beauchamp,
Leicestershire. LE8 0RX
Tel: 0116 279 2299
Email: books@troubador.co.uk
Web: www.troubador.co.uk/matador
Twitter: @matadorbooks

ISBN 978 1785899 775

British Library Cataloguing in Publication Data.
A catalogue record for this book is available from the British Library.

Printed and bound by CPI Group (UK) Ltd, Croydon, CR0 4YY
Typeset in 11pt Aldine401 BT by Troubador Publishing Ltd, Leicester, UK

Matador is an imprint of Troubador Publishing Ltd

To Megan

CONTENTS

A Briefless Barrister?   1

National Service   9

Personal Recollections of Cambridge   34

Cambridge Revisited   51

My Life in the Law   61

Dagenham and Bombay   96

Nationalisation of the Aircraft Industry   137

Immigration Appeals   159

Now it Can be Told   173

Too Old to Learn?   176

Music and Languages   183

Defence of Britain's Imperial Record   196

Sport – Not for Me   211

Postscript – Reflections on the EU Referendum Result   219

A BRIEFLESS BARRISTER?

More than fifty years ago, when I was living in India, I devoted many of my leisure hours to writing a memoir of my five years as an Assistant District Commissioner in Sierra Leone between 1954 and 1959, while I still had a fresh recollection of those years. The memoir was published in 2002 under the title *Remote Corners*. Now that I am in my eighties it seems to me that I have had a very varied and at times exciting life, much of which is just as worth recording as my experiences in Sierra Leone. I have had a wide range of experience from working as a swimming pool attendant, to sitting in judgment on immigration appeals, and from being a humble clerk in the Royal Air Force to a position as Company Secretary of a major multinational pharmaceutical company.

From the age of 20 when I began the study of law at Cambridge, the law has been a constant theme in my life but by no means the only theme. This is a task I ought to have started years ago and after a belated beginning I just hope that I live long enough and continue to enjoy good enough health to finish it. I am confident that although I am writing about events which occurred some years or even decades ago, my recollection has been reasonably accurate. Where it has been possible I have undertaken research to support faded memories. At the outset I must acknowledge gratefully the support and encouragement in this endeavour I have been receiving and continue to receive from my wife Megan, daughter Kamini, brother Robin and younger sister Susan.

I have not sought to write a conventional autobiography,

1

which would be boring. Instead, I have selected a number of events and different aspects of my life and written separate chapters about them. In this way the book takes on the form of a collection of essays and gives the reader the option of selecting those chapters which are of particular interest and exonerates him or her from any obligation to read the book from cover to cover – though I hope of course that the contents will be found sufficiently appealing for any such exoneration to be found unnecessary. The chapters are in roughly chronological sequence, but the emphasis is on subject rather than chronology. As a consequence there is inevitably some overlap between chapters. For example, the chapter on 'My Life in the Law' deals in part with my first steps towards becoming a lawyer which are also covered in 'Recollections of Cambridge'.

My reason for this episodic treatment is that I have had a fragmented though ultimately successful career. Most people would prefer to join one organisation, civil service, commerce or industry and spend the rest of their lives working in it, possibly making some progress and gaining promotion over the years. I was ambitious and impatient of slow progress, so I chose to move on in the interests of furthering my career. It meant personal upheaval every time I changed employer and at times some unhappiness, but overall I can now look back with satisfaction and say that I made worthwhile contributions to some if not all the companies for which I worked and to the other organisations to which I devoted my part-time efforts.

I should mention music as an abiding and lifelong passion from the age of 14 or thereabouts. I started to learn the piano at that age, which was rather late, but I learned quickly and with enthusiasm. There have been periods in my life when I have not had access to a piano, particularly when I was in Sierra Leone, but I have now had a piano at home since 1966 and have long been active in various ways in making music with other people, particularly since retirement in 1992, followed by a move from Surrey to Wiltshire in 1993.

The book's title, *Confessions of a Briefless Barrister*, needs an explanation. It is not merely deliberately ambiguous but in the absence of any explanation would be misleading. A briefless barrister is normally one who is not getting any briefs to act for clients in litigation or advisory work from solicitors or other professional intermediaries and is therefore in desperate financial straits. Such a barrister must normally be in independent practice in chambers in London or a provincial city. But I was never in chambers anywhere and never appeared in court as a barrister. I became an employed barrister while working for Hawker Siddeley Aviation, simply by eating the requisite number of dinners at Gray's Inn, studying in my spare time, and passing the Bar Final examinations. Such a route to achieving professional status as a barrister is no longer open, now that the requirements of being called to the Bar are that as well as eating dinners and passing the Bar Final examinations, a candidate must have undergone some practical professional training and must obtain a practising certificate. So I have never been briefed because I was never in a position in which I would have been professionally allowed to accept a brief. In this sense I was always happy to be a briefless barrister and never had to suffer the penury associated with that unfortunate condition as the expression is normally understood.

I was born on 27 October 1930 in Darwen, a town in Lancashire then dominated by the textile weaving industry. My birth certificate shows that at that time my father was a lorry driver. My mother had been a weaver at Greenfield Mill, where her mother was also a weaver. I was born at 1 Tunnel Street, one of a row of humble terraced houses built in the nineteenth century by the owners for the employees of Greenfield Mill, and still standing and inhabited. I have three younger siblings: a sister, Margaret, born in 1934, a brother, Robin, born May 1940, and a sister, Susan, born 1944. I do not propose to go into detail about my early years, but to summarise, the main events of my life are as follows:

1941-1945: Darwen Grammar School.

1945-1949: Bolton School. At the end of 1948 I was awarded an open scholarship to read modern languages at Corpus Christi College, Cambridge.

1949-1950: Eighteen months national service in the RAF as a clerk, during which I spent over a year in Germany.

1950-1951: Corpus Christi College, Cambridge, reading for Modern Languages Tripos Part I, French and German. First in Tripos Part I.

1951-1953: Corpus Christi College, Cambridge, reading for Law Tripos Part II. BA degree in 1953. Upper Second in Law Tripos Part II.

1953-1954: Appointed as a Cadet Administrative Officer and given a posting to Sierra Leone. Attended the Devonshire Course in London in preparation for service in Sierra Leone.

1954-1959: Service in Sierra Leone as an Assistant District Commissioner. Two periods of home leave in that time, in 1956 and 1958. I resigned from the service in 1959 because of the imminence of independence for Sierra Leone and the realisation that I needed to find a different career.

1959-1960: A brief period of employment with Ford Motor Co. at Dagenham, in Personnel.

10 September 1960: Married Megan and became the stepfather to her two children. This became possible because Megan had spotted an advertisement for a position as Company Secretary to a British-owned company in India. I applied for the job and was delighted to get it.

1960-1964: Service in India with my wife and two stepchildren as Company Secretary to Asbestos Cement Limited, a company 75% owned by Turner & Newall of Manchester, making building materials at four factories in different parts of India. We had home leave from India in 1962, during which we bought a house in Hereford, in Megan's home county. In India, I wrote the memoir of my experiences in Sierra Leone which was later published in 2002 as Remote Corners.

1964-1966: Assistant Company Secretary of the British Aluminium Co. Ltd in London.

January 1965: We sold the house in Hereford and moved to a house in West Molesey, Surrey, just over a mile from Hampton Court Palace. We stayed in this house until May 1993.

1966-1976: Employed by Hawker Siddeley Aviation Limited, first as Legal Assistant, then as Legal Manager from 1968, after I had been called to the Bar, and finally as Executive Director Legal.

1966: Having passed the examinations of the Institute of Chartered Secretaries and Administrators, I was appointed FCIS.

1966-1968: Joined Gray's Inn. Ate my dinners, studied in my spare time, passed the Bar Final examinations and was called to the Bar.

1975-1976: Led the formation of British Aerospace Staffs Association (BASA) and became its first chairman.

1976: I joined The Wellcome Foundation Limited as Company Secretary. At that time the company was wholly owned by the Wellcome Trust, a prosperous charity which funds medical and scientific research.

1984-1985: Chairman of the Bar Association for Commerce, Finance and Industry (BACFI).

1985-1986: Flotation of Wellcome as a listed company on the London Stock Exchange, a process in which I, as Company Secretary, was heavily involved. After flotation the company was now owned only as to 76% by the Wellcome Trust.

1987: Appointed Queen's Counsel.

1992: Appointed as a part-time Immigration Adjudicator. Retired from Wellcome.

1993: Moved from West Molesey to Great Bedwyn, near Marlborough, Wiltshire.

1994: Became a board member of the newly formed Sarsen Housing Association in Devizes, Wiltshire.

1996-2001: Chairman of Sarsen Housing Association.

2002: Retired from my appointment as a part-time Immigration Adjudicator. Became Honorary Legal Adviser to Migration Watch, an appointment which I still hold. Remote Corners, a personal memoir of my experiences over five years in Sierra Leone, was published.

2004: Elected as a pensioner trustee of the Glaxo Wellcome Pension Fund, which pays my pension.

2006: Retired from the board of Sarsen Housing Association.

2008: Retired from my appointment as a pensioner trustee.

I hope that readers will find this chronological summary a sufficient general guide to the contents of the chapters which follow.

Job Hunting

In 1953, I graduated and accepted a Colonial Service appointment. In 1992, I retired from Wellcome at the age of 62, having occupied the intervening years with six very different full-time jobs. I can proudly boast that every move I made from one job to the next was wholly voluntary. I was never dismissed or made redundant. All these moves meant that I spent a great deal of time and energy applying for jobs and attending interviews with prospective employers. I returned from Sierra Leone in 1959, having resigned from the Colonial Service and from India in early 1964, having resigned from my position of Company Secretary of Asbestos Cement Limited in Bombay. On both occasions I came back to Britain unemployed and with no promise of employment from anyone, but on both occasions I was confident that I would find a suitable job in time. The search in 1959 took less than two months, but in 1964, it took eight months. We had come back from India with savings which would keep the family alive for two years with no income and we had a house in Hereford where we could live while I was job hunting. But although the situation was one for which we had adequately prepared, it was still an anxious time. We economised by not having a car or a telephone. Fortunately,

6

the house was not far from Hereford's railway station, to and from which I was able to walk on my frequent day trips to London and sometimes other cities such as Birmingham, Bristol or Sheffield, to attend interviews with prospective employers. I was fortunate in that I was always able to claim travelling expenses for these journeys. On days when I stayed in Hereford, my main occupation was going to the local library to check the 'Situations Vacant' in the *Daily Telegraph* and other newspapers, followed by a session of typing job applications on my portable typewriter. The daily delivery of mail was always an anxious moment. For the most part I applied for jobs in which my experience in Sierra Leone and India might be of some value, and I was hopeful that it might be possible to find employment in or near Bristol, my favourite provincial city, but in the end I had to accept that very few worthwhile posts in which I was employable were to be found outside London. The most exotic position for which I was interviewed was that of Managing Director of Caithness Glass at Wick in the far north of Scotland. I was interviewed in London by a management consultant and had to admit in the course of the interview that I was not really qualified for the job. Megan did not seek to discourage me from going ahead with the application but was not attracted by the thought of possibly having to move to such a remote and distant location, and was thankful that I was not successful. Another senior position advertised at the time was that of Managing Director of Northern Ireland Railways. I was invited to go to Belfast for an interview on the Thursday before the start of the Easter holiday – not a sensible day to choose. All flights from London or Birmingham were booked so I did not go. If I had been offered the job and taken it I might have found myself in charge of the railways there at the beginning of the Troubles in 1969. The railways were the target of IRA bombers from time to time, so in retrospect I do not feel any regrets at having foregone the opportunity to be considered for the post.

Sometimes I attended interviews abroad. In 1975, when I

was legal adviser to Hawker Siddeley Aviation Limited, while it was in the process of being nationalised (see the chapter on nationalisation), I was invited to attend an interview for a legal appointment with a company in Canada. This was difficult, but as it happened I had to visit New York on Hawker Siddeley's business and arranged to fly from there to Detroit, not far from the Canadian border, and a manager from the Canadian company came to collect me. On other occasions, I had to go to Essen in Germany and to Amsterdam.

One of the problems with job hunting was that of having to tell lies to one's employers. Interviews invariably took place on working days so it was necessary to cook up some excuse for being out of the office.

The most important interview I ever had was in the summer of 1960 when I was recruited as Company Secretary to Asbestos Cement Limited in Bombay and in consequence was able to marry Megan and become stepfather to her two children. I have described the special circumstances of this interview, or rather series of interviews, in the chapter on Dagenham and Bombay.

NATIONAL SERVICE

After the end of the Second World War the United Kingdom continued to have major military commitments around the world which necessitated maintaining the numerical strength of the armed forces at a high level. Occupying forces were required for Germany and Austria, defeated nations whose previous armies had been disbanded. Apart from the needs of occupation, the Soviet blockade of West Berlin created the need for the Berlin Airlift to keep the city fed and supplied, and relations with the USSR were hostile and created the need to establish NATO in 1949 as a protection for Western Europe against a possible Soviet invasion – not a fanciful possibility at the time. Apart from Europe, substantial garrisons had to be maintained in Gibraltar, Malta, Cyprus, Egypt, Palestine and Aden to protect the major imperial lifeline to India. British troops continued to provide part of India's garrison until 1948, when the last units withdrew following the partition of British India into India and Pakistan in 1947. Following the defeat of Japan, Britain re-established its colonial presence in Southeast Asia, which meant that garrisons had to be provided in Singapore, Malaya and Hong Kong. Some smaller numbers of troops were needed for duties in British colonies in East and West Africa and there were large bases for the Royal Navy in Hong Kong, Singapore, Bombay (now Mumbai), Trincomalee in Ceylon (later Sri Lanka) and Simonstown in South Africa.

Conscription had had to be introduced during the war and was maintained in modified form after the war so as to provide the manpower to meet all these commitments. Men aged 18 were obliged to spend eighteen months performing national service, usually in the army or RAF, followed by four years on the Reserve, during which they were liable to be recalled to duty for limited periods. My recollection is that the navy was able to manage without conscripts. From October, 1950, the period was increased to two years because of Britain's commitment to support the American forces fighting in Korea following the start of the Korean War. Conscription for national service eventually ended in 1963. It was a huge and costly burden for a country just beginning to recover from the ravages of a major war.

Men who were otherwise liable to be called up could be exempted on medical grounds, or because they were in coal mining, agriculture or other reserved occupations, or because they were conscientious objectors. Taking so much time from the lives of young men meant that for that period they were removed from the labour market or from professional, university or technical education. Men who were going to train to become doctors, engineers or scientists were normally allowed to defer the start of national service until they had finished their training, but no such deferment was allowed for going on to read arts subjects or undertaking legal or other non-technical or non-scientific education or training.

Royal Air Force – Square Bashing

There was no deferment for me, so I joined the RAF on 21 February 1949. I had stayed on at school for an extra term in the sixth form so that I could sit the scholarship examinations at Cambridge in December 1948. The result of these examinations was satisfactory in that I was awarded a Minor Scholarship to read modern languages at Corpus Christi College. Having a birthday on 27 October was convenient, as I was able to leave school in January 1949, complete my eighteen months National Service in September 1950 and take up my scholarship at the start of the academic year in October.

Spending a week in college in December 1948 for the purpose of taking examinations and being interviewed by one or two fellows of the college had been a very exciting culture shock, and reporting for duty on 21 February to RAF Padgate near Warrington in Lancashire was another but less agreeable culture shock. It was a huge camp consisting mainly of wartime huts, each accommodating around thirty beds and was the main reception centre for new national service RAF recruits. I was assigned to one of these huts with a group of other young men of my age, hailing from all over the country and speaking with a variety of regional accents. We had all been passed as medically fit on physical examination beforehand but had to have a further medical check. We were issued with uniforms and other items of kit such as webbing belts, two pairs of boots and ground sheets, which also did duty as waterproof capes. It poured down all week, and as we had to march in the open between our billets and the cookhouse and other buildings scattered around the camp, the ground sheets were invaluable. Towards the end of the week we had to pack all our civilian clothes into the suitcases we had brought with us, which were then sent back to our homes.

The next stage was basic recruit training and for this I was included in a batch of men being sent to Bridgnorth in Shropshire. We were marched in a disorderly column from the camp to a station in Warrington where we boarded a special train to take us to Bridgnorth. Buses took us from Bridgnorth station to the camp on the outskirts of the town where we were immediately taken into the loving care of NCOs who yelled at us to fall in and generally carry out their commands promptly. I found myself assigned to a flight – I suppose the RAF equivalent of a platoon or company in the army – which took up four huts in one corner of the camp, each accommodating thirty recruits. Each of us had a bed with a small wooden locker beside it. The hut was heated by two cast-iron coal-fired stoves. Lavatories and wash basins were in a separate adjacent block, referred to as the ablution block. Like Padgate, the camp had obviously been put up during or just before the war. Soon after we arrived we had to extract knife, fork, spoon and drinking mug from the kit we had brought with us and be marched off to the cookhouse, which I suppose was about half a mile away. Taking charge of the men from the hut to which I belonged was an Irish corporal.

Over the next eight weeks we had to undergo a rigorous and exhausting programme of basic training, not materially different from the sort of training that army recruits would have been given at that time. We had to learn basic foot drill and later an arms drill. We all had old Lee-Enfield 303 rifles issued to us for the purpose of learning how to slope, order and present arms, and to march carrying them. These rifles had all had their firing pins removed and we were not given any ammunition, so we were safe with them. We were all issued bayonets, again for the purpose of a drill, though there was also training in combat with fixed bayonets, which involved charging at filled sandbags suspended on posts, sticking the bayonet in, twisting it to do maximum damage to the notional enemy, all the while uttering blood-curdling yells. We were also given instruction by NCOs in cleaning and taking care of our rifles. The lessons usually began with the words, "This is a rifle – never call it a gun." I have fond memories of a not very bright NCO telling us that we needed to wipe the outside of our weapons to remove what he insisted on calling 'artificial' dust, a malapropism for 'superficial'. Our other encounter with rifles was on a firing range, where we were given the opportunity to use loaded weapons to fire at targets under strict supervision of NCOs who observed the results of our firing through binoculars. When it came to my turn I did not show any aptitude for marksmanship and was reprimanded for firing at the wrong target.

The programme was highly organised and each day was divided into periods rather like a school curriculum. Foot and arms drill took up most of the time, but there were also periods of PT and lectures on subjects such as the organisation and ranks of the RAF and aircraft recognition. Discipline was strict and we had to get used to jumping in response to yelled orders. We had to dress smartly, clean our boots and webbing, polish buttons and fold the sheets and blankets on our beds in prescribed order every morning. We had to keep our huts clean and there were frequent inspections. Another part of the programme was doing fatigues and other general duties. I can recall being sent to do duty in a hut which housed some office accommodation, with the job of cleaning the lavatories, sweeping floors and lighting the stoves for heating. We also had to take turns at fire picket duty, which meant staying up all night fully dressed and patrolling part of the camp. I doubt whether we would have been much use if there had been a fire or other incident, as we were not given any training in fire drill or any other aspect of security. A slightly glamorous duty was that of ceremonial guard at the main gate of the camp, which involved posting two airmen dressed in their best blue uniforms with shining brass buttons and with rifles, one on each side of the gate. We had to observe strict drill routines and maintain set positions throughout, standing at ease or attention with arms ordered, i.e. with the rifle's butt resting on the ground. From time to time we had to perform a synchronised drill – shouldering rifles, doing a smart left turn, then marching a set number of paces to the left, performing an about turn and marching back the same number of paces. I had the duty of giving the order for both of us to start this drill at the same time by banging the butt of my rifle twice on the concrete. If an officer below the rank of squadron leader passed, we had to come to attention, slope arms and salute by slapping the butts of our rifles with our right hands. If the officer was of higher rank we had to come to attention and present arms.

It had rained heavily during our week at Padgate, but for the eight weeks at Bridgnorth it was a pleasant spring, a prelude to the good summer of 1949, so although we had to go through a tough and sometimes exhausting programme of training, the weather was mostly kind to us. We were reasonably well fed, though this was still in the time of post-war austerity. One abiding impression I had from Bridgnorth was that we seldom saw an officer. There was a Flying Officer who commanded the flight I was in and another flight, but he rarely put in an appearance. He gave us an occasional talk and I recall that he led the flight at our passing out parade at the end of the eight weeks, but for the most part all the work of actually putting us through training and maintaining discipline was left to the corporals and the one sergeant who had overall charge of the flight. One incident I recall is that we were all called together one afternoon and told, supposedly in confidence, that one of our number had tried to commit suicide with his bayonet. We were told this by one of the corporals whose admonition to us was "I don't want anyone to take the piss out of X." This was surely the kind of occasion when an officer ought to have visibly taken charge.

A major feature of the shock of national service was that of being thrown into the midst of an arbitrary group of contemporaries from many different parts of the United Kingdom and becoming accustomed to a large variety of regional accents – Scots, Welsh, Northern Irish, Liverpool, London and Geordie. For me it was my first acquaintance with this latter brogue, not readily comprehensible at first in some cases. There was a sprinkling of school leavers and men destined to go on to university after national service, but otherwise they came from a great variety of occupations – butchers, lorry drivers, bank clerks, and many others.

Typewriter Bashing – Clerical Training

We had a passing out parade reviewed by the station commander and accompanied by the station's band. After eight weeks of intensive square bashing we acquitted ourselves well and immediately went off on a week's home leave. In the course of our time at Bridgnorth we had all been interviewed and assessed for suitability to careers which would take up the rest of our service. There was not much that could be done to train young men for any very skilled job when they were in uniform for only eighteen months, so for the most part they became clerks, cooks, drivers or storekeepers. One or two who were destined to go on to higher education were selected to go on to officer training, but the possibilities in that direction were limited for the same reason. Clearly, the RAF needed pilots, engineers, aircraft fitters and mechanics; occupations which called for long periods of training. For these the RAF had to look to volunteers prepared to join for a career of at least several years. In the course of my own interview I was judged not to have officer-like qualities – the official jargon used – and was assigned to a clerical training course. For this I went to the RAF's clerical training school at Wythall, outside Birmingham. This was another camp of wartime huts.

It was an intensive training course, but mainly sedentary, learning about the clerical routines and procedures which would be part of our daily duties and also learning to type. We learned, for example, the correct paperwork to be issued for sending airmen or officers on leave and how to record postings, promotions, leave and other events in what were called Personnel Occurrence Reports or PORs. I recall that we had to be familiar with the special procedure for sending Irish personnel to the Republic on leave. Ireland had remained neutral during the war and although many Irishmen and women joined British forces this was officially frowned upon by the authorities in Ireland, so any Irish personnel from the Republic going home on leave had to be sent first of all to a particular station where they would be issued with civilian clothes. I never actually had to comply with this instruction. This was long before the days of computers or electric typewriters, so we were trained on manual typewriters. We became familiar with the layout of the keyboard and practised typing exercises to special music designed to ensure that we maintained a regular speed. I can say in all honesty that touch typing was a skill which I learned and used in the RAF and which has served me in good stead ever since. At the end of the course there was a written examination which tested what we had learned over the six weeks, as well as our ability to type at a reasonable speed.

To Germany – Lübeck

After clerical training came postings to units at which we would start work. We were all invited to volunteer for overseas postings, which some of us did, contrary to the advice of all the old sweats among the regular airmen who would tell young recruits that they should never volunteer for anything. Having volunteered I was selected, and on the day before the course ended I sent a telegram off to my parents saying: "Posted overseas. Home tomorrow on embarkation leave." I had a fortnight's leave in Darwen and at the end of it reported to an RAF Transit camp at Hednesford in Staffordshire, knowing that I would be going abroad but not where. Those of us who were in the same intake were told on a parade that our destination was Germany, which certainly pleased me as I would be going on to read French and German at Cambridge after national service. We were issued with various extra bits of kit such as a pocket knife and a pair of webbing gaiters, which neither then nor at any later time had any apparent practical significance for a posting to Germany.

We were allowed a weekend's leave and on return were all put on a train together for London's Euston Station, where we were allowed a few hours at liberty before joining another train at Liverpool Street for Harwich, where we boarded a ferry doing duty as a troopship. We all had bunks on one of the ship's lower decks and the ship sailed overnight to the Hook of Holland. We disembarked the following morning and had a good breakfast in an army restaurant on the quayside before boarding a special train to take us across the Netherlands and into Germany. The sun shone and it was a pleasant journey. I confess that at the time I was woefully ignorant of European geography and only had the vaguest idea of where we were heading.

The train took us to Bückeburg, near Bad Eilsen, where British Air Forces of Occupation (BAFO) had its headquarters. Bückeburg is a historic town in Lower Saxony, previously the capital of a small princely state, with a 700-year-old castle, Schloss Bückeburg, now a museum. At the time it was a garrison town mainly for the RAF and along with Bad Eilsen had not been damaged by the war. I was told by an officer who had had war service that Bomber Command had been instructed to avoid bombing this area and certain others which were planned to be occupied by British forces of occupation when the war ended. I did not have the opportunity to make better acquaintance with the town, as I was posted after two days from there to Lübeck, travelling there by train through Hamburg. The station to which I was posted was St. Hubertus, a small town a few kilometres south of the city and close to the RAF air base. Lübeck and its surrounding country were in the state of Schleswig-Holstein, in the British Zone and part of West Germany, but very close to the frontier with the Soviet Zone, East Germany. The air base had been one of those used by the RAF to operate its planes to Berlin to keep the city supplied during the airlift. The airlift had recently ended because the Soviets had abandoned their blockade and reopened the roads, railways and waterways connecting Berlin across the Soviet Zone with the British and American Zones of West Germany.

The station to which I was posted was occupied by two units, both concerned with supplying technical services in the form of building works and machinery repairs. It had been a German army barracks and was set in very pleasant forest with solidly built permanent barrack blocks, offices and other buildings spaciously laid out. The living accommodation was far superior to the wartime huts to which I had become accustomed at Padgate,

Bridgnorth, Wythall and Hednesford, the four RAF stations which I had passed through up to this point. I shared a barrack room with three other men and had to walk just a hundred yards or so across parkland to station headquarters where I worked. I was on the staff of the station adjutant, a flight lieutenant, and my immediate boss was the orderly room sergeant, a regular NCO with some years' experience. The staff was a mixture of airmen and German civilian clerks, all of whom of course spoke excellent English. Now I began to learn how to put into practice some of the procedures I had recently been learning, though there were also jobs for which my training had not prepared me. The working atmosphere was pleasant and friendly and I soon began to use my German to chat with the civilian staff. This was just over four years after the end of the war through which all of them had lived and in which some had done military service, but I never detected any feelings of animosity towards the occupying Brits. For a while I shared an office with a young German woman who was engaged to be married and intending with her husband to have a honeymoon in what was then referred to as the East Zone, the Soviet Zone which later became the Deutsche Demokratische Republik (DDR). She was a bit nervous about this, though in the event she happily survived the experience.

In the evenings and at weekends we were able to travel by bus from the main gate into Lübeck. As members of the occupying forces, if in uniform we travelled free. The city as an important port had been heavily damaged by air raids during the war but many of its historic buildings, in particular the Holstentor or main gate with its twin towers and the Rathaus (town hall) had survived intact. An important personal milestone for me in Lübeck was a visit to the city's opera house for a performance of Wagner's *Tannhaüser*. Like most German cities and large towns Lübeck had and still has its own opera house. Up to that time my only acquaintance with live opera had been one or two performances in Bolton or Manchester by the Carl Rosa Touring Opera Company of *La bohème* and

Il trovatore, so the chance to hear Wagner for the first time was very exciting. In the centre of Lübeck there was a small lounge-cum-library for the use of visiting servicemen and on a visit there I was able to read a synopsis of *Tannhaüser*, so I went along to the performance having prepared myself to some extent for the evening. I do not suppose the performance was anything special but I was bowled over by the sheer power of the music more than anything else, the overture and Pilgrims' Chorus, the Venusberg Music 'Dich teure Halle' and other numbers.

Göttingen

Life at St. Hubertus was pleasant enough. The routine of work and barrack room life was not too strenuous, we were fortunate to live and work in attractive forest surroundings in comfortable accommodation and were well fed. But I felt that I ought to be able to make better use of German and had a chat with the orderly room sergeant on the subject. He put up a case for me which went to BAFO (British Air Forces of Occupation) headquarters and resulted in my being posted to headquarters at Bad Eilsen, near Bückeburg, which I have already mentioned. Bad Eilsen, as its name indicates, is a spa town and some of its main buildings had been requisitioned by BAFO. One major hotel had been converted into the main headquarters office building and another one was the officers' mess. Accommodation for airmen and airwomen was in prefabricated huts of a far superior quality to that of the wartime structures in the camps where I had been stationed in the United Kingdom. None of the buildings which formed the headquarters were fenced off from the rest of the town, so the German civilian population mixed with the airmen and women and soldiers in the town. I recall that there was a guard room where the RAF Police kept a check on movements of personnel and vehicles, and right next door to it was a German pharmacy. I had been assigned to the Intelligence Section of headquarters and on reporting there I was told that I would be off on detachment to a unit called the RAF Employment Unit in Göttingen, so my stay in Bad Eilsen was just two nights. I travelled to Göttingen by train and was met at the station by a car driven by one of the officers. I was bowled over by the new station to which I had been posted. The unit was accommodated in a large, requisitioned solidly built house in a smart area of the city, near a large area of woodland – 81 Herzberger Landstraße, an address I can never forget. In 2010, Megan and I had a holiday in Germany which included three days in Göttingen and I was able to show her the house, still there and now occupied by a doctors' surgery.

The unit's cryptic title was meaningless. It had been set up by RAF Intelligence to interview German Prisoners of War still being belatedly repatriated by the Soviets more than four years after the end of the war. Those with homes in West Germany were handed over at a crossing point with the Soviet Zone at Friedland★, a few kilometres from Göttingen. They might have

★A brief history of the transit camp at Friedland is given in *The Times* for 5 April 2016. The story states that the camp was established by the British Army in September 1945 for displaced Germans. It was used for housing up to 4000 of the many thousands of migrants arriving in Germany in 2015 and is currently being used as the first arrival point for the refugees Germany has been taking under UN supervision from camps in the countries neighbouring Syria. I quote from the article:

Friedland has been maintained as a purpose-built facility on permanent standby for humanitarian crises. Once the final German prisoners of war had returned from the Soviet Union in 1955, the camp played host to refugees from Hungary in 1956, Chile in 1973 and Vietnam in 1978. Since then, four million migrants and displaced people have been through the camp, including Tamils from Sri Lanka, Albanians and Iraqi Christians before the latest influx of Syrians.

been held as prisoners for up to eight years and had in many cases spent time as more or less slave labourers at one or other of the many Soviet air bases in European Russia or Siberia, where they might have been able to observe movements or other activities which were of interest in building up a picture of Soviet military activity and strength. Interviewing these men, the Heimkehrer as they were known, was the task of the four or five officers who made up the unit. They were all flight lieutenants and were all fluent in German and all of them had had war service. The army had a unit which did the same job, but we never had any contact with them. At the time when I arrived at the unit there were more Heimkehrer arriving every day, so there was plenty of work.

What made the unit remarkable and probably unique was that it consisted of several officers and just two airmen, a driver and a clerk (myself). The officers had to write reports on the interviews they carried out and it was my job to type the reports on stencils. This was long before the days of copiers or other rapid means of multiplying copies. Stencils were made of wax-coated paper and were fed into the roller of the mechanical typewriter. The typing of the copy was undertaken with the typewriter ribbon disconnected, so that the keys cut into the paper and made an impression. The complete stencil would then be used to produce multiple copies on a Gestetner duplicator. The duplicator had a rotating drum which was first coated with special black ink before the stencil was fixed to it and a stack of plain sheets of paper was placed underneath, pressed against the drum so that when the drum was rotated by hand it pressed the stencil against each sheet of paper in turn and pushed it out of the machine. In so doing it printed onto the paper the text which had been cut into the stencil. In fact, I did not have to do the duplicating myself, but I sent off the typed stencils to Bad Eilsen for duplicating and distribution of the copies. Apart from this task I dealt with correspondence, typed letters, kept files, and answered the telephone. I had not learned shorthand, so if officers wanted me to type their letters they had either to write them in longhand for me to copy or dictate them at a suitably slow speed. As a further note on the contemporary technology of making copies, it was normal when typing letters to make carbon copies. Special carbon paper was placed under the top copy with a sheet of copy paper underneath. Sometimes up to four or five copies could be made simultaneously and the whole bundle was fed into the typewriter. When the top copy was typed the typewriter keys made an impression through the carbon paper onto the copies below the top. This was a means of making only a very small number of copies at a time. A bundle of too many copies would be too thick to feed in and in any event the lower copies became progressively fainter and more smudged.

81 Herzberger Landstraße had obviously been the home of a prosperous family. It had a basement and three floors above it and was clearly designed to be occupied by a family who could afford servants, which meant that it was readily adaptable to the needs of the RAF unit which occupied it. The basement had a large kitchen, larder and servants' dining room, which was used at mealtimes by the driver, myself and occasionally by RAF or army visitors below commissioned rank. On the first floor, reached by imposing steps from the entrance gate, there was a spacious lobby and there were three reception rooms. One had been converted to an office which I shared with the officer who did duty as adjutant. The other two rooms were the officers' dining room and lounge. The lounge had a splendid grand piano which I was able to play occasionally when all the officers were out. The next floor up consisted of four or five officers' bedrooms and the top floor had one more officer's bedroom and a bedroom obviously intended to be occupied by one or more servants which I shared with the driver. The house had no garage, an indication that it had probably been built towards the end of the 19th century. There was, however, ample space for cars between the front gate and the road without trespassing on the pavement.

The house had a big garden at the back and round one side. We were looked after by German civilian staff recruited locally and paid for, I believe, out of occupation costs imposed by the occupying allied forces on the German populace. In charge was a majordomo by the name of Willi Gagelmann, who had I think been an officer in the Wehrmacht. The only other men were one of the cooks and a boilerman who looked after the central heating and various odd jobs. There was a female cook, a waitress called Elfriede for the officers' dining room, and two young women, Ursula and Gisela, who made beds, did the cleaning and performed other menial tasks, including most memorably that of delivering early morning cups of tea in bed to officers and airmen alike. Willi spoke good English but the rest of the staff spoke only German. As all the officers and I also spoke German, that became the daily language of the house. The driver had in the course of service in Germany picked up a limited few phrases of colloquial German and when necessary I translated for him.

Life as a national service airman had provided for me up to that point a civilised but fairly austere regimen and in the normal way that would not have changed for better or worse for the remainder of my service. Suddenly being switched into this relatively luxurious environment was a piece of unbelievable good fortune which it took some time to get accustomed to. Most of my days were spent just inside the house. I slept on the top floor, went down to the basement for three substantial meals a day, and worked in the office on the ground floor.

As the driver and I were the only two RAF other ranks in Göttingen, arrangements were made for us to be paid by the army, so every fortnight or so we took a long walk to the nearest British Army barracks and were paid in cash by an army accounting officer. It is an ironic commentary on the problems that Britain was then having with its balance of payments that British service personnel in Germany, there as the occupying force in a defeated nation, were not paid in Deutsch Marks but in a special form of sterling currency issued presumably by the Bank of England. This currency could be used only at NAAFI* clubs, shops, cinemas or other such centres run for the benefit of service personnel. It was possible to buy Deutsch Marks at the official rate of exchange, but there was a thriving black market which offered a much better rate. The German economy was still recovering from the privations of the war and the immediate post-war period, so it was possible for service men and women to sell cigarettes, boot polish, clothing and other items which could be bought from the NAAFI at favourable prices to German civilians at something between official and black market prices.

In my off-duty hours I was able to go into the town, just a short walk down the road. Göttingen had been fortunate during the war in that it did not offer any major targets for the allied bombers and apart from some damage to buildings near the station it had survived the war intact. It was and is a pleasant university town with about 26,000 students. In its centre, now mostly pedestrianised, is a market square with a town hall on one side and a statue of the Gänseliesl or goose girl, a character in one of Hans Christian Andersen's stories, in the middle of the square. On another side was the NAAFI club for soldiers from the local British garrison, whose entertainment needs were also served by one of the town's cinemas, taken over by the army for showing English language films. A great joy for me was the local opera house, also just a short walk down the road, which I regularly visited and where I first made the acquaintance of Verdi through performances of *Aida* and *Un ballo in maschera*. There were performances of entertainments other than opera, such as *Die Fröhliche Witwe* (*Merry Widow*) and Goethe's *Torquato Tasso* as well as satirical reviews which I also attended. On Sunday evenings there was often a symphony concert. This was all very good for improving my German. On one of my visits to

*NAAFI – Navy Army and Air Force Institutes – an organisation providing canteens and other facilities to service men and women.

the opera I became friendly with a young German called Werner who was a few years older than me, worked as a bank clerk, had had war service and spent some time as a prisoner of war in England. He spoke some English, but our regular language was German. He lived in an apartment with his parents and I started regularly visiting them all at home every fortnight. It was odd to reflect that just a few years earlier we had been on opposite sides in a devastating war; Werner had pleasant memories of his time in England and we became close friends. Another event which I recall was attending a lecture open to the public given in English by T. S. Eliot at the university. He was at the time at the height of his fame as a poet, but I am sorry to admit that I have not the slightest recollection of the subject of the lecture.

I was entitled to a fortnight's leave from Germany and decided to save it for the spring weather of the early months of 1950 rather than take at least part of it for going home for Christmas. When I was in the sixth form at Bolton School in 1947 and 1948, two German boys had come to the school for a few months from a school in Cologne. One of them, Hans, had spent some of that time as a guest at my home in Darwen and I had an invitation from his family to spend Christmas with them in Cologne. I travelled from Göttingen to Cologne by train. I had seen something of Germany's war-damaged cities in Hamburg, Lübeck and Hannover, but now saw much more in Cologne, where not a single street seemed to have escaped some measure of destruction. Cologne Station is on the Rhine, next to the cathedral, and I vividly remember seeing the bridge which carried the main railway lines collapsed into the river. Germany was beginning its post-war recovery and the government of the newly established Federal Republic of West Germany had been elected in the summer of 1949, but reconstruction was a huge task and the population was for the most part still enduring austerity and privation. I was made welcome by Hans' family, who though reasonably well off were still living an austere life and welcomed the presents of a cake made by my mother and a tin of good coffee, which I was able to take with me. The family had a piano and a friend of Hans played the violin, so I was able to join in the fun by accompanying him on the piano. The two men were able to invite one or two girls of their acquaintance for a fairly sedate but enjoyable party. The Rhineland region around Cologne is predominantly Roman Catholic and Hans was involved in charitable work organised by the priest at the church which he attended. While I was there the priest and the boys whom he had got together for the purpose organised a collection of small Christmas presents to be collected and distributed among needy local families – of whom there were plenty. The presents were loaded into small handcarts and taken to the addresses of the families selected for these surprise Father Christmas visits. I went with them and was slightly embarrassed at the start of the proceedings to be thanked for my participation by the priest, though I had not in fact contributed anything.

Back in Göttingen it was soon spring and I vividly recall in early May 1950, millions of *Maikäfer*, May bugs, forming a crunchy carpet under the street lights at night. Sixty years later on a private visit to Göttingen, also in May, there was sadly no longer any sign of these insects, though I noted that in the window of a shop selling a tempting range of goodies there were large chocolate *Maikäfer* displayed. One Saturday night in June we had a party thrown by the officers for the German staff and the two airmen. There was dancing and for a while I had Ursula sitting on my knee. She was a lively girl with ambitions to become a professional dancer, ambitions which I suspect were never achieved.

Berlin

The following Monday morning I received an order to move forthwith to RAF Intelligence in Berlin. I admit that by this time the flow of Heimkehrer to be interviewed at the border crossing had declined to a trickle, so there was no longer the same amount of work for me.

So I packed up my kit, said goodbye to friends and acquaintances in Göttingen and went by train to Berlin. The airlift had now long ended so there was now normal traffic across the East Zone between West Germany and West Berlin, partitioned into three occupation zones: American, British and French. The Soviets insisted that British military trains crossing the East Zone must travel at night, presumably as a precaution against the possibility that daytime travel might allow some Soviet military installations to be seen by British servicemen. I was fortunate enough to be allocated a sleeper berth for the journey, in a two-berth cabin which I shared with an army corporal in the Intelligence Corps whom I had met in Göttingen.

My billet in Berlin was relatively luxurious and privileged, though not in quite the same intimate style as I had enjoyed for some nine months in Göttingen. I was assigned to RAF Intelligence in a large ex-German government building in the British sector of the city, which was shared with a miscellaneous selection of other military and British Control Commission for Germany (CCG) units. The standing of this unit was obviously higher than that of the RAF Employment Unit, as the senior officer was a wing commander, assisted by one squadron leader, two flight lieutenants and a warrant officer, the RAF equivalent of a sergeant major. All were fluent German speakers and the Warrant Officer, who had spent part of the war in the Arctic ports of the USSR, also spoke Russian. I was the only airman and there were two German civilian drivers. Berlin, a city divided into four occupation sectors, American, British, French and Russian, in the middle of the East Zone, was an obvious centre for a great deal of espionage, and the purpose of the unit was to interrogate any German civilians who had potentially useful information to offer about Soviet air force installations and activity in the East Zone. The officers often came to the office in civilian dress so as to maintain some measure of secrecy and to disguise the fact that they were serving officers. My job, as in Göttingen, was to type their reports, run them off on the duplicator and distribute copies to various official addressees in Berlin and London. An unusual feature of the office was a Cyrillic script typewriter, sometimes needed to record the registration letters of Soviet aircraft which one of the unit's informants might have seen.

I was accommodated in an 'other ranks' mess some distance from the office, sharing it with men from various army units who had jobs in the same building in which I worked. The most senior was a corporal, who as he was in the Royal Artillery had the rank of Bombardier. For going to and from work we could use a special bus operated for British civilians who worked for the CCG. As an alternative and at other times we could use the Berlin U-Bahn and of course in uniform we travelled free. The mess was in the basement of a modern building. We all had individual rooms and the use of a dining room and bar. The mess was managed by a male German and lavishly staffed with cooks, waitresses and others. The standard of accommodation and dining was probably similar to that of a sergeants' mess. So I settled happily into the life of a city-dwelling commuter for the few remaining months of my period of national service.

West Berlin, the American, British and French occupation sectors, took in the greener and smarter areas of the city, such as Grünewald and Gatow, the latter being the RAF base on the outer edge of the city, up against the frontier with the East Zone. The Olympic Stadium, built for the 1936 Olympic Games, was in the British sector and its tennis courts and other facilities were available for use by British personnel. I went there to play tennis once or twice. The Soviet Zone to the east included the main parts of the city centre, the Brandenburger Tor, Unter den Linden, Alexanderplatz, the Pergamon Museum and the opera house. It also included the industrial and working class areas. One Sunday, a group of us decided to visit the Red Army's huge memorial garden at Treptower Park. This involved first a ride on the S-Bahn and a dramatic view from above of huge areas of the most devastated areas of the city. Then we had to take a long tram ride, still in the British sector when we started but continuing into the Soviet sector. Although Berlin was a divided city, this was long before the infamous wall was erected in 1962 to stop the citizens of the communist east escaping to the wicked capitalist west. However, by early 1950 there were already two separate German states, the Bundesrepublik in the west and the Deutsche Demokratische Republik (DDR) in the east. They already had their own separate currencies, so at the sector boundary one tram conductor taking fares in West Marks had to hand over to a colleague who collected East Marks. We were all in uniform so we travelled free. Treptower Park contained and still contains a huge Red Army cemetery, dominated by a more than life-size statue of a grieving Russian mother. I visited it again in the late 1980s when there were still two Germanys, the DDR still occupied by Soviet forces. On another visit to Berlin after the reunification of Germany it was apparent that Treptower Park had ceased to be treated as a major place for tourists to visit.

The building in which we had our mess was close to the boundary between the British and American sectors and occasionally we wandered over in the evening to the Schloßstraße and had drinks in a café favoured by American soldiers. We were welcomed and they insisted on buying our drinks, which I found embarrassing. Two members of our mess went to the café in civilian clothes one evening and when they came back one of them was laughing hilariously at a trick he had played. One of the Americans was in some sort of trouble and the café had been visited by two American military police who were questioning him. This man put on a fake upper-class British accent and told the police that he was a British officer and was prepared to vouch for the good behaviour of the American soldier whom they were investigating. The policemen naively took the man at his word and were most deferential. They saluted him and offered him a lift in their jeep, which he sensibly declined. If they had asked for identification, which they surely ought to have done, they would have called on their British counterparts to come and arrest the man and his companion and he or perhaps both of them would have been on the serious charge of impersonating an officer.

The Korean War began on 25 June 1950 while I was in Berlin and three months before the end of my national service. Korea, like Germany, saw the end of the Second World War as a divided country, the north occupied by Soviet forces and the south by the Americans. Northern forces invaded the south and before long American, British and other forces landed in South Korea pursuant to a United Nations resolution, and a bitter and destructive conflict raged until mid-1953 when an armistice was negotiated. The division of the Korean peninsula persists to this day and a demilitarised zone marks the frontier between the two countries. The war had the characteristics of both a civil war and of a proxy cold war between the communist and capitalist nations. The Chinese army entered North Korea in support of the regime and General MacArthur, commanding American and allied forces in the south, showed signs of wanting to chase the Chinese out and if necessary invade China. This ambition famously resulted in his being dismissed from his post by President Truman and being given a hero's welcome by the citizens of New York when he made a triumphant progress through the city. As a result of the Korean War, in which Britain was involved and in which British troops fought, the period of national service was increased from eighteen months to two years, an extra imposition which I was happy to miss.

West Berlin was already a major focal point of the Cold War, a capitalist island in the middle of a communist ocean, with recent memories of Stalin's attempt to starve the western city into submission and surrender, which led to the Berlin airlift to keep the city supplied. There were inevitable apprehensions that the Korean War could evolve into something much worse, possibly the Third World War, and Berlin was the most uncomfortable place to be. If the Red Army had been ordered to take over West Berlin, the allied garrisons would very soon have been overwhelmed. Happily the Soviets were not disposed to stir up trouble in Europe, so the status quo of Berlin was not disturbed.

My next visit to Berlin was in 1984, when I was Company

Secretary of Wellcome. For some years the board made an annual visit to one or other of its major subsidiaries and in 1984, the German subsidiary Deutsche Wellcome had the honour. We were based at a hotel in Hamburg for the few days of the visit and the hotel was the venue for the strategic board meeting which was a normal feature of the annual visits as well as for various business and social gatherings with senior German managers and staff and civil servants involved in the oversight of the pharmaceutical industry in Germany. At the chairman's insistence we took time off for a day visit to Berlin, just a short hop by air. By 1984, the city had experienced twenty-two years of being divided by the wall. A small bus had been hired with a local guide to show us the main sights of the city. The high spot of our tour was going into East Berlin through the Invalidenstraße checkpoint – the street being named after a hospital. This was the most formidable frontier crossing I have ever experienced anywhere in the world, all to allow us to pass from one side to the other of the same German city. At the entrance to the checkpoint there were two sections of concrete wall, each blocking half the road and forming a slalom, built to make it impossible for vehicles intent on escaping the east to make a quick getaway. Next there was a concrete wall with a barrier manned by the Stasi, the East German security police. Once through the barrier we were in a kind of no man's land, a space between two high concrete walls, occupied only by a single-storey office building which was the police station. On one side of this space there was a side street which was obstructed by huge concrete anti-tank blocks, again put there to make escape impossible. Our guide had to hand over a list of all the people on the bus and the details were meticulously checked by the police before we were allowed to enter the Soviet sector.

Our guide was able to go with us but he was not allowed to show us the sights of East Berlin, so for this purpose we had to take on an East Berlin guide. The main attraction of East Berlin was the Pergamon Museum and I had my second visit to the Soviet war graves cemetery at Treptower Park. In conversation with our East Berlin guide, he admitted that the residents of East Berlin were enthusiastic viewers of West German television. He was obviously a little embarrassed about the wall, which dominated the eastern half of the city and frequently came into view as we toured. He sought to cover his embarrassment by referring to it as 'the State frontier'. At the end of the tour we came back to the Invalidenstraße checkpoint and this time had to be subjected to a much more thorough inspection by the Stasi to make sure that we were not attempting to smuggle anyone out of East Berlin. The list of names was again carefully checked against passengers on the bus. The bus had its own toilet which was checked to make sure that no one was hiding inside. The Stasi had a special mirror mounted on wheels which was rolled underneath the bus to make sure that there was no one hiding there.

In the time I worked for Air Intelligence in Berlin the flow of informants from the east who were keen to earn a little money by passing on useful information to us diminished and eventually there was little or no work for me to do – not that this mattered because by early August 1950 it was time for my national service to end. I was officially on the strength of RAF Headquarters in Germany and had been on detachment first in Göttingen, then in Berlin, so the first step of being demobilised was to return to my unit at Bad Eilsen. This meant another overnight train journey back into the British sector of what was now the Federal Republic of West Germany. Leaving the Headquarters unit on a demobilisation posting meant that I had to obtain clearance from a whole list of departments to ensure that I was not leaving behind any unpaid debts or other liabilities. I was allowed about ten days for this purpose, far longer than I needed, so for much of the time I was just at a loose end. Fortunately, it was a good summer and I was able to enjoy the park and gardens of Bad Eilsen. One of the people who had to sign my clearance form was the unit's padre, a Church of England clergyman in RAF uniform. He asked me about my faith and I was obliged to tell him that I had none. He became most incensed at this and his reaction was almost that of regarding my atheism as a serious disciplinary matter, one that would perhaps have justified my being charged with 'conduct prejudicial to good order and discipline' to use the familiar catch-all legal expression. However, there was nothing he could do about it, so he signed me off with an ill grace.

So at the end of August 1950 I completed my national service and returned home for a few weeks before going up to Cambridge to begin my three years there as an undergraduate. On the whole I had found national service an enjoyable experience, particularly as I had spent over a year in Germany, getting to see something of the country and improving my acquaintance with its language. The work was not very demanding, but it gave me a familiarity at a very junior level with the routine of office life. I have always regarded myself as a born bureaucrat, so it was a good start. The most useful thing I learnt was touch typing, a facility which I am using in typing this memoir and which I have always found valuable.

One ironic aspect of my national service which is worth mentioning is that although I was in the RAF I never went anywhere near an aircraft; in fact not one of the stations to which I was posted even had a runway. RAF Bridgnorth, like one or two other stations, had a decommissioned fighter as an ornament at its main gate, but that was the nearest I ever got to an aircraft. Although I joined nearly four years after the end of the war, the RAF was still a substantial force and had a considerable administrative tail, dealing with recruit and trade training, intelligence gathering and providing headquarters for RAF units in Germany – to name just those activities in which I was briefly involved. I suppose national service as we all knew it could be regarded by those of us who were going on to tertiary education as the precursor to the modern gap year, the important differences being first that it was a legally imposed obligation rather than a personally chosen long holiday, secondly that it meant work and third that it was modestly paid.

PERSONAL RECOLLECTIONS
OF CAMBRIDGE

Going up to Cambridge in 1950 after eighteen months' national service in the RAF was an exciting experience but meant being plunged into a wholly unfamiliar environment of which I had had just a brief foretaste in December 1948, when I spent a week in Cambridge for the scholarship examinations. Even with the broadening of my horizons by thirteen months in different parts of Germany, it was a huge jump to move from a life spent for the most part until then in a Lancashire mill town to the sophisticated environment of an ancient university city. It was a new and unfamiliar world, inhabited by strange creatures speaking a very different language from that to which I had always been accustomed. Many of my neighbours were from the same kind of background as myself, indeed four of them were from the same school, but others came from august establishments such as Eton or Oundle or were scions of Britain's landed gentry. The last of the ex-servicemen undergraduates with war service were still in residence and the presence of these mature men, older than the rest of us, was a reminder of how lucky we had been not to have been old enough to be called for national service during the war.

In retrospect, a very strong impression is that of austerity; although the war ended in 1945, it took a long time for life to get back to something akin to what we understood pre-war normality to have been. There was still food rationing and undergraduates had to carry their own butter and sugar into hall at meal times. College fare was limited. A dish which made its frequent appearance on the menu for dinner was strong-smelling jugged hare, which I loathed. In common with some of my contemporaries I made a practice of signing out for dinner on any night when jugged hare was on the menu and we would go to Lyons Corner House in Petty Cury – an establishment long since vanished – for a cheap and more palatable alternative. Most of us had to manage on modest incomes, in my case a Minor Scholarship from the college plus a government grant, providing a total of £300 a year or thereabouts, from which to meet the cost of board and lodging in college, books, miscellaneous expenses in term time and the cost of travel between home and college at the beginning and end of term. Unlike students nowadays, we were happily spared the burden of having to meet the cost of tuition fees. I owned few clothes and wore the same pair of corduroy trousers every day of term. We all bought second-hand undergraduate gowns, a compulsory item of everyday dress for undergraduates, which had probably never been dry-cleaned and were often ragged.

College rooms did not have the benefits of central heating or en-suite bathrooms. We managed with gas fires and numerous trips in the course of the day to distant communal bathrooms and lavatories. I followed the common practice of a weekly bath, which meant walking in pyjamas and dressing gown through the grounds of the college, calling for some stamina in the winter.

A striking feature of the life I began to lead was that of being looked after by bed-makers, porters and other college servants who were respectful and deferential but never servile. We ourselves were respectful and deferential in our turn towards Fellows and others whom perforce we had to accept as our elders and betters – though it was possible to be on reasonably friendly first-name terms with Fellows. It would never have occurred to us to rebel even though we might have had legitimate grievances. We had grown up with the discipline of home, school and national service, and acceptance of authority, whatever our private views might be about those in authority, came naturally. We had to consider ourselves fortunate in that we had survived the war and were privileged to be able to undergo the civilising influence of a Cambridge education.

Another abiding impression is that of leading a quasi-monastic life. The college gates were locked at 10pm, though admission could be gained up to midnight by ringing for the porter on duty. All visitors, especially women, had to be out of college by 10pm, though this was a fairly meaningless restriction for most of us in view of the extreme shortage of women in Cambridge. There were only two women's colleges at the time, Girton and Newnham, and their populations combined with those of the women students at Homerton Training College and Addenbrooke's Hospital Nurses' Home produced a ratio of nine men to every woman or thereabouts. For most of us term time was a period of enforced celibacy.

The Quality of Teaching

The general belief was at the time that Oxford and Cambridge offered the finest possible education available anywhere and we were all influenced by that belief, even though sometimes it did not seem compatible with daily experience. I read Modern Languages Tripos Part I and Law Tripos Part II. Lectures in the former were often of indifferent quality and I gained a first in the Tripos in spite of choosing to miss most of them. Law was a different matter. There was a vast amount of detail to absorb and there was a need to make sure that one had some acquaintance with new decided cases and statutes which had not yet found their way into the law books, but to which the lecturers would usually draw attention. It was not a good idea to skip any lectures, even though the standard of lecturers varied a lot. Some of the lecturers simply regurgitated the text book with a bit of minimal updating, but there were others who were famous in their field whose lectures it was a privilege and a revelation to attend. I have in mind particularly Professors Lauterpacht, Wade and Hamson, outstanding authorities in their respective fields of international, constitutional and comparative law.

A great character who would certainly not count among outstanding lecturers but whose lectures on criminal law were nevertheless memorable was Henry Barnes, sometime Fellow of Sidney Sussex, who died more than fifty years ago. He belonged to the now extinct breed of Anglo-Irish Protestants, a graduate of Trinity College Dublin and a British patriot, convinced of the supreme greatness of Great Britain and Ireland before partition. I remember one of his oft repeated sayings as "These two islands are the centre of the world and everybody has offices in London." It was said that in his younger days he had been something of an adventurer and had become involved in politics, to such an extent that he briefly became President of a South American Republic. However, he was warned by one of the generals that it would be in his best interests if he left the country forthwith. He took this advice, made his way back to the United Kingdom and Cambridge and somehow or other became a law lecturer. This part of his life story sounds too bizarre to be true, but it was confirmed after his death by his obituary in *The Times*. Even as undergraduates many of us realised that the content of his lectures was not wholly reliable, though it was undoubtedly entertaining. He had a habit of quoting cases which no one else had ever heard of and to which one could certainly not discover any references in the text books on criminal law. His summary of the facts of a particular case would often begin with the words "Now this fellow got a girl into trouble," uttered in a pronounced Irish accent and repeated on so many occasions that we all cheered each time.

Somehow or other, although he was lecturing on criminal law, he deviated on one occasion into telling us about the origins of the law of trusts. Knights going off to the Crusades wanted to have some dependable body or person to look after their estates in their absence. This meant a transfer of ownership and the obvious bodies to accept this responsibility were the monasteries. However, the monasteries were forbidden by their vows of poverty to accept such transfers. This obstacle was circumvented by transferring title to the land to some lay person 'to the use of the monastery', so that the lay transferee did not acquire a beneficial title. The monastery could however enjoy the benefit of the land in the absence of the original owner. Henry Barnes's explanation of this ended up with the memorable words, "You see, the subtlety of the clergy."

His most unforgettable summary of a criminal case related to a man who was convicted of bestiality with an animal, to wit a duck, but according to Henry Barnes, "The Court of Criminal Appeal quashed the conviction because they said that a duck was not an animal." What an outstanding lawyer I might have been if I could have remembered the contents of all the hundreds of law lectures which I attended as well as I remember that particular sentence. He became a legend in Cambridge and in recent years I have met several contemporaries who were lawyers and retained vivid memories of Henry Barnes.

Undergraduates at Play

Another entertaining recollection which I have of Cambridge relates to a variety show at one of the theatres at the end of the summer term 1953, just when the Tripos examinations were ending and the undergraduates were ready to let their hair down. At the time, of course, the Lord Chamberlain still exercised his powers of censorship over theatrical performances, powers which were eventually abolished by the Theatres Act 1968. The Lord Chamberlain's most notorious and arbitrary rule was that nudes were permitted on stage, but only if they did not move. Word soon got around that in this show there were indeed nudes and certain of the more affluent undergraduates – not including myself, I hasten to add – decided that this was an opportunity too good to miss. They bought tickets for the front rows and boxes and went along to the theatre armed with water pistols, said to be capable of firing as many as thirty-two shots without needing to be refilled. When the curtain was up and the nudes were on stage holding their statuesque poses these undergraduates took aim at the girls and managed a few direct hits. My recollection is that the girls were mindful of the need to comply with the Lord Chamberlain's edicts and not bring the company or the theatre into disrepute, so they stoically maintained their poses while cold water trickled down their naked bodies; one or two of them may have unavoidably shuddered a little, but it was hardly perceptible – or should I say *barely* perceptible. These antics led to a great deal of uproar in the house and there were protests from some of the townspeople in the audience, who objected to having their evening's entertainment hijacked in this way. After a few disrupted scenes the curtain came down and the manager came onto the stage. His message was, "If this behaviour continues I shall bring down the curtain and give everyone their money back – except members of the university." The message was heeded.

Another incident which I vividly recall is the rustication of Mark Boxer*, sometime editor of the student magazine *Granta*. The proctors, officers of the university with

*He was the first person to be so punished since Shelley was sent down from Oxford. The Vice-Chancellor had demanded that he be sent down but King's College, of which he was an undergraduate, succeeded in reducing the sentence to a week's rustication in May Week. The novelist E.M. Forster (long a resident of King's College) spoke in his defence. The punishment meant that he missed the College's May Ball. However, May Balls go on into the small hours, so Boxer made a triumphant return at midnight. After he graduated he became editor of *Lilliput* and later was founding editor of the *Sunday Times* colour supplement, creating a format which other newspapers copied. At the time of his death in 1988 he was editor of *Tatler*. He was twice married, the second time to Anna Ford the television newsreader (Source – Wikipedia article on Mark Boxer.)

responsibility for student discipline, took offence at a poem which he published in *Granta*, including the line 'God is a bit of a sod', which they considered blasphemous – I think in the summer term 1953 – and they made an order for his rustication in May Week, which as everyone knows is the first week in June. He organised a spectacular send-off for himself. He hired a local undertaker to turn up on King's Parade on a Sunday afternoon with a horse-drawn hearse, a coffin and attendants in black with top hats and the usual regalia. In attendance also were an undergraduate dressed in the trappings of a Roman Catholic priest and numerous acolytes similarly attired. One of Mark Boxer's friends stood on the hearse and delivered a mock funeral oration on the demise of the editor of *Granta*. The 'priest' walked along King's Parade swinging an incense burner dispensing huge clouds of incense and intoning mock Latin prayers in which the word 'granta' frequently and audibly occurred. It was a great piece of entertainment. It was a hot afternoon in early summer and Cambridge was crowded with tourists who greatly relished this free unexpected spectacle. For some time KP was completely blocked with crowds of undergraduates, townspeople and tourists, all enjoying themselves. It would be inconceivable nowadays that the proctors would take such stern disciplinary action for what would certainly be regarded as a minor offence or more likely would not be considered an offence at all.

Vacation Time

Students from less prosperous homes and even those a bit better off have always spent at least part of their generous vacations working to earn a bit of cash. Like so many I used to help with the Christmas mail or do other odd jobs near home. In the 1952 Long Vacation my father through his local government connections arranged for me to spend a few weeks working as a swimming pool attendant at Morecambe's open air baths. I ascertained that they were opened in 1935 but have not been able to find out whether they still exist. They were on the seafront and took in and filtered salt water from the sea. The pool was of generous dimensions and was, I believe, the largest open air swimming pool in Britain at the time. I do not think the water was heated but it nevertheless managed to attract large numbers of bathers during the summer holiday season.

I have never been a particularly strong swimmer and I fondly imagined that I would be somewhat overshadowed by other attendants with beefy muscles and lifesaving qualifications. We were of course all temporary staff taken on for the summer months during which the pool was open. I was horrified to discover that of the half dozen or so men safeguarding bathers on the side of the pool there were only two of us who were not drawing old-age pensions. The pool was open for long hours in the summer, so we had to work in two overlapping shifts, with the result that for a few hours of my shift I was the only employee on the side of the pool who might reasonably be expected to jump in and rescue any swimmer in difficulty. Fortunately, our numbers were strengthened by a few younger people after a week or so.

There was a resident variety company providing entertainment twice a day in the open, including a bevy of girl synchronised swimmers. I had to admire their stoicism in braving the chilly water daily and performing elaborately choreographed routines. On one occasion one of the girls developed cramp in one of her legs and two of us had to go in and lift her out of the water. I got my trousers wet up to the knees and never felt tempted to enter the water again all the time I was there.

An event which drew large crowds of spectators was the weekly bathing beauty contest. The position I usually occupied on the side of the bath was alongside a platform which jutted out

41

into the water and provided a stage for all the entertainers. The girls taking part in the contest would parade on this stage and stand in a line, facing sometimes towards me and sometimes with their backs to me. On chilly afternoons I was often treated to a view of a line of quivering bottoms popping out of skimpy swimsuits.

The pool had the usual diving boards but also one special temporary tower which, if memory serves me right, was ninety feet high. It had been made for a film of four of Somerset Maugham's short stories, one of which was about a woman high diver performing for the public. The high spot of one of the daily shows was a dive from this tower by a member of the company, accompanied by suitably dramatic noises from the organist, who played a cinema organ providing music for the show.

On one occasion the pool was invaded by a group of young men who had been drinking and were running around, making a lot of noise and indulging in rough play, generally making a nuisance of themselves. Some of them went out onto the platform and started jumping into the water near other bathers. This obviously called for some action so I, as the nearest attendant, walked onto the platform and asked them to desist. One of them began to argue with me and was moving slowly from left to right foot with a swaying and turning motion. I realised just in time that his intention was to push me into the water, so I took quick avoiding action. The organist, from his station across the pool, told me afterwards that everyone was eagerly waiting for the splash.

On the side of the pool which I patrolled the bathers walked in down a gentle slope whereas on the other side there was a pathway raised above the level of the water from which bathers either dived in, jumped in or climbed down steps set in the side of the pool. This meant that the path on my side was at water level and there were drains all the way along so that the path did not become flooded. By a masterpiece of civic planning the town's gasworks, producing coal gas, were directly across the road from the baths. Polluting exhaust smoke from the process regularly settled on the water at the edge of the pool, forming a black film, so it was part of my job to go along the side with a broom and sweep the dirty water into the drains. One Saturday afternoon my mother, two sisters and grandmother came to visit me and sat on the seats at the side of the pool. Some of the time while they were there I was busy sweeping, which caused my grandmother to burst into tears with a cry of, "That poor lad, after all that education!"

During the few weeks I spent working at the swimming pool the number of temporary employees taken on to patrol the side of the pool increased and most of them were of my age group, which I found reassuring. Some of them did not show any great enthusiasm for the odd jobs such as sweeping up or moving poolside furniture and tended to spend an unconscionable amount of time chatting to the girls taking part in the show. Being a fairly conscientious sort of chap, I did not care to spend too much time in the company of obvious loafers, so when I was meant to be working I made a point of keeping clear of others who were also meant to be working but clearly were much more interested in socialising. We did however have tea breaks in a cafeteria with French windows looking out onto Morecambe promenade and a grassy bank close to the pool building. One afternoon when a group of us were having a tea break we observed a young couple enjoying a spot of slap and tickle on the grassy bank, clearly oblivious to the fact that we were able to observe them closely in broad daylight. They were romping around vigorously with the result that the girl's short skirt rode up round her waist revealing an absence of knickers. Such are or were the joys of seaside summer holidays, even in a North Lancashire resort.

Morecambe is about thirty miles from my hometown Darwen, so I stayed in lodgings with a family while I was there, a middle-aged couple with an adult daughter named Elsie. I felt

43

rather sorry for the father, whose life was ruled by these two domineering women. Elsie was somewhere between 25 and 30 and had been married, but her marriage had been dissolved for reasons which I never learned, by what her mother insisted repeatedly on calling a '*degree* of nullity'. She had a good singing voice and regularly took leading parts in local amateur musicals. Sometimes in the evening I was able to accompany her on the piano. She did not appear to have any current serious men friends and I began to form the impression that she was quite keen on me, particularly when she suggested that I might like to 'team up' with her, as she put it, so that we could go touring together as a musical partnership – hardly a realistic possibility. Having seen her father suffering at close quarters I made a point of ensuring that I did not give her any encouragement. One Saturday evening she went off to a dance in the town and dropped hints that I might like to go with her, but I did not rise to the bait. When she came back she told me that I had not missed anything, which made me feel even more sure that I had taken the right decision in staying in the house to read a text book on criminal law in preparation for the next term at Cambridge.

The French Press

Corpus Christi College administered a fund with which it had been endowed by the Lazard family, of the investment bank. The family had had a son at Corpus and owned a vineyard in Normandy. The endowment provided money for an annual scholarship to be awarded to undergraduates who had obtained good results in French in the Modern Languages Tripos. On the strength of Firsts in French and German in Part I of the Modern Languages Tripos in 1951, I was awarded a scholarship worth £60, a goodly sum at that time. The conditions of the scholarship required me to travel to France, study some aspect of French life or culture and write a report about it on my return. I accepted the recommendation of my tutor in Modern Languages, Patrick Charvet, that I should study the workings of the French Press. Charvet arranged for me to meet the editors and other members of staff of *Le Figaro* and *Le Monde* in Paris and of a leading provincial newspaper, *Les Dernières Nouvelles d'Alsace* in Strasbourg. He also arranged for me to meet and have lunch with *The Times* Paris correspondent, an old member of the college.

I spent most of September 1951 in France, dividing my time between Paris and Strasbourg. I still have a copy of the report which I wrote, forty-two pages and about 10,000 words. I had to have it typed so that one copy could go to the Lazard family and another copy be lodged in the college's library. From rereading this report it is apparent that my time in France was very much a working holiday, visiting newspaper offices, talking to editors and others, collecting and studying numerous books and publications which were my source materials. The French press in 1951 was recovering from particularly difficult years of occupation and division of the country between German occupiers and the Vichy regime. In the occupied zone there had been a burgeoning of clandestine Resistance newspapers, one or two of which, notably the communist *L'Humanité*, survived the war and became established national dailies.

Strasbourg was not exactly a typical French provincial city, being the capital of a Department which between 1870 and 1945 had been seen by Germany as rightfully belonging to it and had been formally annexed by the Third Reich after the occupation. In 1951, it was still very much a German-speaking region and the newspapers were published in both French and German. Nowadays French is dominant. The German legacy remains in that whereas French trains other than the Paris Metro travel on the left, in Alsace they travel on the right.

Hitchhiking Across Europe

The early post-war years were a time of austerity and this meant among other things that students wishing to take advantage of the freedom of travel, something we had all been denied during the war, had to do it on the cheap. I can recall some of them boasting in newspaper articles that they had travelled huge distances in continental countries thumbing lifts from passing drivers of cars and lorries and sometimes enjoying meals and other benefits from their peripatetic hosts. I had a superior variant of this kind of holiday during the long vacation in 1952, after my period of working as a swimming pool attendant. I did not belong to any social circle of men or women whom I could readily join to go on holiday and I was wholly unfamiliar with the world of travel agents who by then were busy offering package deals to Spain and elsewhere. I had travelled to France with a school party in 1947 and on my own in 1951, so I took it for granted that if I wished to go anywhere I would have to go alone. In the undergraduate newspaper *Varsity* I saw a small advertisement for a fairly cheap holiday in Andorra, a tiny country sandwiched between France and Spain of which I knew nothing. So I booked it and set off on my own, travelling all the way by train, in particular having a long overnight journey sitting up in second class from the Gare d'Austerlitz in Paris to Latour-de-Carol in the Pyrenees. From there it was a long journey by bus to my destination in Andorra. This was a small hotel in a small town on the main road between Spain and France and I realised as soon as I arrived there that I had made a mistake. I had a bedroom with just a bed and bedside table. There was no cupboard, just a nail for hanging clothes in the back of the door. There were other people staying there, mainly French, but it was apparent that there was very little to do there, other than perhaps taking a trip to Barcelona. My heart sank at the dismal prospect of spending a few days there.

The hotel had a roadside restaurant advertising *'repas à toutes heures'* and an American driving alone stopped for a meal. His name was Khent Haupt and as I was the only other native English speaker in the restaurant I started talking to him. He belonged to the publicity department of Esso in its New York headquarters. Esso used to publish road maps given away free at petrol stations selling its branded petrol and Khent's job was to drive around France, Spain, Italy and Switzerland checking on how up-to-date the maps were and on the general level of service at Esso's franchised filling stations. He had decided that he had driven enough for one day and would stay the night at the hotel. My disappointment and dismay at my poor choice of holiday resort led me to ask whether he would give me a lift back into France the following day. Perhaps that would now be considered impertinent, but it was in keeping with the customs of the day, certainly so far as students were concerned. What I had in mind was a lift back to Latour-de-Carol and from there to use my return train tickets home.

So the following morning I checked out of the hotel, whose manager was not at all pleased that I was cutting short my stay and collected from me some compensation to which he referred as a *'forfait de chambre'*. Although I had asked only for a lift back into France, Khent invited me to travel with him for a while. Clearly for him, as an American travelling through countries with which and with whose languages he was not at all familiar, it was a lonely job and he was grateful for company. Also I could speak French and German and was enough of a linguist to pick up some basic Italian when that became necessary. So we travelled across the south of France and beyond, visiting lots of parts of France, Italy and Switzerland, which for me, as for others of my generation, were exciting and exotic. I can recall the thrill of seeing the Mediterranean for the first time. Khent and I both greatly enjoyed viewing girls in bikinis, then all the rage as a splendid post-war fashion innovation, displaying their almost naked bodies nonchalantly on the beach at Cannes. We crossed the frontier from Menton to Ventimiglia, my first visit to Italy.

In Italy, Khent had to visit Esso's Italian offices at Genoa, which meant that I was left on my own for a few hours. I had lunch at a restaurant where I had to choose from a menu in Italian only, listing unfamiliar dishes with equally unfamiliar names. Later in the journey I became used to visiting smaller restaurants in the south where the waiters would simply invite us to choose spaghetti, macaroni or whatever other pasta was available. But this was a major city in the sophisticated north. It really was a case of pointing to a dish as my choice and hoping it would be something palatable. In fact my choice may well have been rabbit, not a personal favourite. I had the added embarrassment that I was in scuffy shorts and jacket, being served by waiters in smart white jackets and shirts with bow ties. In spite of this they were friendly and polite. Later, we made a brief stop in Milan, where at least I briefly saw the cathedral. Then on to Venice, where we took a two-day break at a small *pensione* on the Lido, where Khent was calling on some American friends. We left the car at the Piazzale Roma car park and took the passenger ferry to the Lido. We were not sure of the whereabouts of the *pensione*, so I summoned up my best improvised Italian to ask a young woman sitting by the roadside, *"Scusate Signoruna, ma dovè si ritrovai la il albergo Verdi?"* She smiled and answered in a middle-class English accent, "I'm sorry, I don't speak Italian."

At that time Britain's balance of payments problems meant that private travellers were allowed a yearly maximum of £25 to spend in foreign currency. This maximum was my total wealth on the journey and even if the allowance had been more generous, impecuniosity, the normal condition of a student, would have prevented me from taking advantage of it. I had made reasonable efforts to pay my way while travelling with Khent, though I was acutely conscious that in increasing measure the costs of this trip made in comfort through some of Europe's main tourist areas in the height of summer were being met as charges against Khent's Esso expense account. I was able to assuage feelings of guilt by the realisation that I was able to help Khent as an interpreter and travelling companion, but even so decided that it was probably time that we parted company. Venice was an appropriate point for us to go our separate ways, as I could take a train from there to Paris, from where I could use my return tickets to travel all the way back home to Lancashire. I put this to Khent, but after considering the matter, he invited me to keep him company on the next stage of his otherwise lonesome journey, which would take him down to the south of Italy and back again. I happily accepted the invitation.

From Venice we travelled down the east side of Italy as far as Taranto then back up the west side, passing through many towns and cities, including Amalfi, Positano, Naples, Rome and Florence.

We crossed into Switzerland at Chiasso, and from then on I was able to help Khent as an interpreter in German, being then still fluent in the language. Khent was on a business trip and in any event was never too interested in conventional sightseeing. When we were heading towards Naples I was map reading and he asked me where a road joining on our right was from. I told him it was Pompeii, to which he just said, "Guess we don't see Pompeii." I would dearly have loved to visit Pompeii, but as a hitchhiker I could hardly ask for a time-consuming diversion, so I just swallowed my regrets at what we were missing. Khent was, however, keen on seeing some of the twentieth-century's engineering achievements. At this time motorways had been built only in Germany and Italy, but in France he made a point of driving along the Corniche when we passed through the Riviera. In Italy, he made sure of using the Amalfi Drive and later called at the Ferrari factory in Modena to see something of their sports cars being built. In Switzerland what attracted him was a journey on the Jungfraubahn, Europe's highest railway. We were fortunate in that the sky was cloudless and at the Jungfraujoch we had a clear view of the glacier and of other mountains. Also, we were able to step outside into the snow.

We finally parted company at Zürich. Khent bought me a train ticket from there to Paris and generously gave me fifty dollars to see me comfortably back home. He had earlier given me one of his Esso maps of Europe on which I marked the route we drove and all the places at which we stopped. I still have the map as a valued memento of a wonderful journey. He was a few years older than me and had had wartime service in the American merchant navy as a radio operator. We were much in each other's company on the road and in hotels and restaurants for over a fortnight and talked of everything under the sun. I kept up correspondence with him for some years afterwards, though we never met again.

CAMBRIDGE REVISITED

Over the years I have been back to Cambridge many times and for many different, usually social, reasons. Corpus Christi College affords its alumni the privilege of dining on High Table and I took advantage of this in 1956 when I was home on leave from Sierra Leone. It was interesting to hear the sort of conversation Fellows of a Cambridge College have among themselves. One of the College's most famous old members is the Elizabethan dramatist Christopher Marlowe, whose time as an undergraduate is commemorated by a plaque in the Old Court. Speculation about the person who really wrote the plays of Shakespeare has been going on probably since the bard died and at the time there was some excited discussion of an impending visit to Cambridge by an American academic who had been propounding the theory that the plays had been written by Marlowe. Obviously, the visitor was expected to call at the college and the Professor of Anglo-Saxon, one of the Fellows at High Table, commented that "the college should keep its fingers crossed." I do not recall that there was much publicity about this visit when it occurred or that the American academic's theory ever had much impact.

I have never understood why so much detailed painstaking research and the efforts and labour of so many gifted scholars should be devoted to the vain task of trying to prove that the plays of Shakespeare were in fact written by someone else. Why forego the fame and pleasure of having written the works of the greatest poetic and dramatic genius ever by having them assigned to a non-existent contemporary under a pseudonym?

Why should Marlowe, for example, himself no mean dramatist, lay claim to the works of a contemporary who is acknowledged to be the greatest of all poetic and dramatic geniuses? To propound such a theory is to assume that Marlowe, having established his own reputation with *Dr. Faustus, Tamburlaine* and other great dramas which survive and are still read and performed, should go on to write and have performed another thirty seven even greater plays under a pseudonym, denying to himself the glory and fame already linked with the name Shakespeare at the time? Furthermore, this would have been a truly astonishing achievement when one takes into account the fact that Marlowe died at the age of twenty nine in a tavern brawl.

One of the younger Fellows, a lecturer in Natural Sciences, had just returned from a visit to the United States and his colleagues were interested in hearing of his flight back to the United Kingdom, transatlantic air journeys being at the time still a rare experience. Someone else cracked what was apparently an academic joke. "Have you read the works of Professor Tannenbaum?" "No, what did he write?" "I have no idea." For some reason this was considered hilarious and the story was capped by the Professor of Anglo-Saxon who said that he had indeed read the works of Professor Tannenbaum in nine volumes. My immediate neighbour was another Professor, in the Modern Languages School, who asked me about my work. I told him that I was on leave from Sierra Leone and this prompted him to ask, "Is that somewhere near Lourenço Marques?" (The former colonial name of Maputo, capital of Mozambique.) Sierra Leone is a Spanish name originally, but might also be taken as Portuguese, and Mozambique was a Portuguese colony, all of which might explain why the learned Professor thought he was asking a percipient question. The most polite answer I could make to his question was that Sierra Leone was indeed in Africa but some thousands of miles from Lourenço Marques.

In September 1962, when I was on leave from India with Megan and the children, I had an invitation to a McCurdy Dinner at the College. McCurdy was a generous benefactor who had provided a fund for an annual dinner for old members of the College. Another more recent benefactor was Beldam and each year invitations are issued to old members who matriculated in specified years to attend either a McCurdy or a Beldam Dinner. I cannot remember exactly, but the invitation in 1962 may have been for all old members who matriculated between 1949 and 1955. As time goes on and the ranks of graduates are thinned out by death, the time span of years whose graduates are eligible for invitations inevitably increases. The invitation I received in 2011 was for old members who had matriculated before 1960. These are grand and enjoyable occasions and the scope of hospitality provided extends to free accommodation in undergraduates' rooms in college. Before dinner there were drinks for everyone in the garden of the Master's Lodge. In 1962, the dinner menu was up to the usual high standard – the wines were excellent, the tables in hall were lit by candles and the college silver was on display. The College drinking horn was passed around and the usual ritual of standing in turn to take a sip of mead from it, bowing to one's neighbours, was observed. We were all in dinner jackets and the fellows wore their gowns. There were of course no women present. Several of my friends and contemporaries who had graduated with me in 1953 were present and we talked until late in the night, exchanging reminiscences and telling each other about our post-graduation careers and personal lives.

An invitation in 2011 which I accepted was a sad occasion by contrast. At the age of 80, I had to face the fact that all but two of my closest friends from my undergraduate days were dead. One of the two still alive was living in the United States, the other in Australia, and neither was able to make it to the dinner. There were indeed drinks in the Master's garden, but there were no waiters going around topping up the champagne. The college is nowadays in more straitened times and hospitality is no longer on the lavish scale hitherto enjoyed – not even it seems at dinners which are paid for from benefactors' endowments. In hall I found a place among men of my year, whom I dimly remembered. The atmosphere was generally congenial and the conversation was civilised, but none of my neighbours had ever been a close friend. In accordance with tradition, after we had finished the meal and before the port was passed round there was a break in which anyone who wished to move to a different part of the hall and talk to other people was invited to do so. It was by now after 10pm and I took advantage of the break to leave the hall and go off to bed. Again in accordance with tradition, breakfast was available in the hall on the Sunday morning from 8am. I am always awake early so I skipped breakfast and left as soon as I was ready, collected my car from a nearby car park and was on my way home long before 8am.

At the end of that experience I decided that I would not accept any further invitations to college feasts. In 2015, I was invited to attend another McCurdy Dinner on 26 September. By now all my contemporaries whom I could reasonably describe as friends were dead and much as I would have enjoyed the excellent food and wines I wrote to the President to decline with regret. I told him that I was just coming up to my eighty-fifth birthday and was rather touched to receive a personalised birthday card signed by the Master – an honour I never had before. I also received this year an invitation to the annual dinner of the Nicholas Bacon Law Society. The cost of the dinner would have been £70 and as it took place in term time I would not have been able to have a room in College, so I would, out of necessity, have stayed in a hotel. But if I had otherwise found the prospect of attending the dinner pleasurable I would not have minded the expense.

Fundraising and other Events

In the early 1990s the college embarked on an ambitious development plan which involved increasing and improving undergraduate accommodation, building a new lecture theatre, and creating a new library and study centre for undergraduates. Properties on Trumpington Street which were always owned by the college had had their lower floors let to a bank and various other tenants, while just the top floor was used for undergraduate rooms and was separately accessible from staircases inside the college. All the tenancies were now terminated and the space thus made available was converted into college accommodation. The Eagle Hotel★ in Benet Street on the north side of the college belongs to the college and the new lecture theatre was built in its grounds.

Obviously these plans were going to need substantial sums and a major fundraising effort was launched, concentrating particularly on alumni perceived to be affluent. As Company Secretary of Wellcome I was obviously considered to be in this category and was approached by one of my contemporaries who had become Chairman of a major company and asked if he could come to see me. I invited him to lunch at the office and after lunch he made a lengthy and detailed presentation of the college's plans, assisted by photographs and diagrams. The important message came right at the end when he advised me in polite and carefully chosen words that he and the other members of the college committee which was undertaking the task of fundraising had assessed my ability to contribute at £50,000. This came as something of a shock. I was well paid

★The Eagle achieved an important place in recent history as the pub to which Crick and Watson went from the Cavendish Laboratory across the road to have a drink to celebrate the major scientific breakthrough of establishing the composition of the molecule of deoxyribonucleic acid (DNA) on 28 February 1953.

and comfortably off, but I was in no position to make that kind of gift to my old College or to any other deserving cause. I was by now Queen's Counsel and it seemed at least likely that this fact had influenced the assessment. A QC in private practice, particularly at the commercial bar, could certainly at that time be earning hundreds of thousands annually, but I was in employment, earning a good salary but not at that level. I had to tell my visitor that I had been seriously, albeit flatteringly, misjudged. He went away disappointed. I sent the college a cheque for £1000 which was gratefully acknowledged.

The College has always held annual events which are open to old members. Usually the pattern is that one year there is a dinner in hall just for old members and the following year there is a summer garden party at Leckhampton, the college's luxurious hostel for postgraduate students just off Grange Road, beyond Selwyn College. This is always a far more attractive prospect because it is held at lunchtime, no formal dress is required and spouses are welcome. I soon gave up attending the dinner, mainly because it was always the same few contemporaries who turned up. But Megan and I regularly attended the garden party, much more informal and with a wider choice of company. Also, Leckhampton has extensive grounds, including a rose garden and open air swimming pool – a most enviable place for postgraduates to live. Sadly, however, the deaths of so many of my contemporaries and of all the Fellows of my acquaintance who also used to attend have greatly diminished the attraction of the occasion for us and we no longer go.

Probably about thirty years ago the college started its own Nicholas Bacon Law Society, open to law students and to old members who are lawyers. In 1988 or thereabouts, I accepted an invitation to attend the Society's Annual Dinner at the college, an event which was attended by about twenty people. Events such as garden parties and dinners were always held in vacation time. But the Nicholas Bacon Law Society was managed mainly by and for the benefit of undergraduates, so its annual dinner was held on a Saturday night in term time. I was allocated a room in college and was bowled over by the realisation that the days of an all-male college were over and there were now large numbers of women among the undergraduates. Women were very much in evidence as part of the normal population and several of them attended the dinner. It was a Saturday night and there were plenty of parties going on and numerous rooms in which the main occupation seemed to be watching television. This was not Cambridge as I remembered it. In my day television was only just getting restarted after the war and one of my first recollections of television was watching the Queen's Coronation in 1953 after taking the Law Tripos Part II.

We had drinks before dinner and one of the other guests introduced himself to me as Sir Murray Stuart-Smith, a High Court judge. (He later went to the Court of Appeal.) As it happened he was the judge who had just finished hearing a major product liability case in which Wellcome was the defendant. The issue in the case was the extent if any to which Pertussis (whooping cough) vaccine could cause brain damage to babies who were injected with it. It was alleged that the plaintiff, a child, had suffered brain damage in his early years and that this was brought about by the negligence of Wellcome who had manufactured the vaccine. The judge ruled that as a preliminary issue medical and scientific evidence should be heard for the purpose of determining whether the vaccine in question could be shown to be capable of causing brain damage. This required the presentation of large quantities of learned scientific and medical papers and the oral hearing of much expert evidence on both sides. It required the clearing of a courtroom in the Royal Courts of Justice, removing the hundreds of volumes of law reports which normally filled the shelves and replacing them with vast numbers of bulky files and bound volumes of medical and scientific journals. Nowadays, making such voluminous evidence readily accessible in a courtroom would be achieved simply by installing the requisite number of computer terminals, having previously input the requisite data. The trial of this issue lasted for some months and at the time when I met Sir Murray the hearing had ended and he was still in the process of considering the vast amount of evidence which had been presented and had not yet written his ruling on the preliminary issue. I explained to him that as Company Secretary of Wellcome I was responsible for *inter alia* the conduct of litigation to which the company was a party. The case was of major importance to the company and I had taken a close personal interest in it, including spending some time in court while evidence was being heard. It was therefore obvious that we should not discuss the case, so we refrained from doing so.

My next contact with the Society was some years later in London, when I was invited to a dinner at the Reform Club by another High Court judge, Sir Terence Etherton, who was also an old member of Corpus and launched an appeal for funds to set up a number of scholarships for law students. With the disappearance of government grants to help students through university and their replacement by loans, this was a worthy cause, a means of enabling students from less prosperous homes to finance their law studies. I happily contributed £1000. I continued to receive invitations to attend the Society's annual dinner and decided this year, 2014, that I would again accept. I am sorry to say that this was not such a happy experience as the previous occasion. College rooms were not available so I stayed in a hotel, the former Garden House Hotel by the river, now renamed as the Doubletree by Hilton. The first dinner described above had been a pleasant and reasonably intimate occasion at which the numbers were just enough to be accommodated in one of the smaller dining rooms. The dinner in March 2014, was a huge affair with over 100 people attending, so the function filled the hall. At 83, I was by far the oldest person present, treated politely and with a certain amount of curiosity by some of the law undergraduates to whom I spoke before dinner. I confess that I felt like a historical relic and no doubt my interlocutors felt the same about me. They were truly astonished when I told them, for example, about having to take our own butter and sugar into meals because of rationing, about having to wear gowns when out on the streets of Cambridge in the evening and the college main gate being closed at 10pm. It was an excellent dinner with a superb choice of wines, and I was placed at table in the company of two of the college's postgraduate law students who were pursuing obscure legal historical subjects involving investigation into ancient court records, the sort of task I would have found insufferably boring. It sounded to me like the sort of research undertaken by graduates who either cannot find a suitable career or who are scared of the outside world and are prepared to accept a life of genteel poverty and near destitution to remain in the cloistered comfort of academia. All my contemporaries are now dead and if I were to go back to Cambridge for any function I would be among complete strangers. I shall not risk it again.

In the course of my years as Company Secretary of Wellcome, I twice organised secretariat conferences as a means of bringing together lawyers, trademark and insurance specialists, and others from Head Office and from Wellcome's subsidiaries around the world. The second of these was planned for April 1992, and I decided that Cambridge would be an ideal venue. I made a booking for the conference at the Garden House Hotel (that was still its name then), possibly the best hotel in Cambridge at the time on an idyllic site by the river. The hotel has its own place in the post-war history of Cambridge because in 1968 or thereabouts it hosted a party of Greek politicians at a time when Greece was ruled by a junta of colonels, with the result that the hotel was attacked by a party of undergraduates as way of showing their disapproval of the visitors. For the purpose of preliminary planning, I visited the hotel with Christine Dunkerley (as she then was, before she became Christine Sherwood on remarriage), a highly efficient assistant. All was set, but my plans were thrown into chaos by the decision of the Wellcome Trust to organise a further sale of their shareholding in Wellcome plc in 1992. I had to cancel plans for the Cambridge conference, though I was able to organise a replacement event in October 1992, my last month with the company, in a hotel in the centre of Windsor. By this time I had ceased to be Company Secretary, having handed over responsibility to my successor and was simply a senior executive without portfolio.

MY LIFE IN THE LAW

I made a late start as a lawyer, not being called to the Bar until I had reached the mature age of 37. I was never in private practice, but managed to be appointed Queen's Counsel in 1987 at the age of 56. As a barrister I never served a period in pupillage or otherwise worked under the supervision of another lawyer and never joined a set of chambers. Hence, as explained in the opening chapter, my irregular and unconventional assumption for the purposes of the book's title of the designation of briefless barrister.

Cambridge

Languages were my first love and I went up to Corpus Christi College Cambridge in 1950 with a Minor Scholarship to read French and German. I was pleased to gain a First in Part I of the Modern Languages Tripos at the end of my first year. This was as far as one could go in the study of the languages and Part II would have meant studying the literature of the two languages for two years. Nowadays, Part II would mean studying a much wider range of cultural and other subjects relevant to the countries in which the languages are spoken and spending some time in those countries, but the academic enlightenment which led to this was still some years ahead. I was confident of my ability to acquit myself well in Part II but was concerned that unless I achieved my primary ambition of a post at an appropriate level of seniority in the Foreign Office or Home

Civil Service (which sadly I did not) I might be condemning myself to the unwelcome prospect of a teaching career. Teaching modern languages – French in particular – at secondary school level to apathetic and sometimes even hostile British pupils did not appeal. To qualify myself as a potential university lecturer would have entailed obtaining a doctorate by means of two years' research into some obscure corner of French or German literature and writing a long and unreadable thesis. University teaching aroused no greater degree of enthusiam than teaching in a secondary school. I therefore decided to take advantage of the flexibility which Cambridge allows and read for the Law Tripos Part II instead. I admit that I was influenced by the example of one of my contemporaries in the college who was also reading modern languages and had decided to switch. It was a bold decision, but one which I have never had cause to regret.

Reading law was much more arduous than reading modern languages, as I have mentioned in the chapter on 'Recollections of Cambridge'. I achieved an upper second in the Tripos, which was a respectable result. Failure to achieve my primary ambition to enter public service in the United Kingdom was a serious blow and led me perforce to accept the much less attractive prospect of the Colonial Service, as I explained in my first book, *Remote Corners*. I would gladly have pursued the alternative of a professional career in the law, but at that time with no financial backing of any kind that alternative was not available. Getting established at the Bar was always difficult and still is. Solicitors in those days normally required cash payments to take on articled clerks and expected them to work unpaid. Garth Moore, my Director of Studies, suggested that it might be possible to find a firm of solicitors which would *give* me articles, but when I asked him how I would live while thus employed he had no answer.

So I joined the Colonial Service and went to Sierra Leone. A law degree was certainly useful to me there (as noted in *Remote Corners*). When I began to contemplate leaving to find employment in the United Kingdom, inevitably I thought about joining Gray's Inn to start a belated apprenticeship at the Bar. I might have been able to make some progress in that direction by eating dinners as required by the Inn when I was on leave, but the financial barrier, the problem of supporting myself and my family while studying for the examinations remained. In 1960, I took up an appointment in India as Company Secretary to a British-owned company, and the background of a law degree plus experience of working in a partly legal capacity in a territory which in 1961 became independent as a fellow Commonwealth member, certainly were important factors in getting me the job. I left India in early 1964 and was after a period of unemployment appointed Assistant Secretary of British Aluminium, a substantial company in its day but long vanished. Again, my accumulated experience helped and was material to some aspects of the work I did as Assistant Secretary, but the financial barrier to becoming a barrister remained.

Hawker Siddeley Aviation

I had a most fortunate break in April 1966, when I joined Hawker Siddeley Aviation Limited with the ponderous job title of Legal Assistant to the Executive Director Contracts, the late Eric Jenkins. He had advertised for people to work in contracts, so I responded to the advertisement and was offered the post of his Legal Assistant which I gladly accepted. I had read law at Cambridge for two years and had had much involvement in legal matters as a colonial civil servant and as a Company Secretary in India, but I was not a lawyer and could hardly believe my good fortune. I was very happy with HSA in this capacity from my first day until I moved on ten years later. Within a few weeks I was asked to involve myself in drafting a contract between HSA and Rolls Royce for the engines to be fitted to the Nimrod maritime reconnaissance aircraft which was to be built for the RAF – a transaction worth many millions and of much importance to both companies and to the RAF. Looking back on that task I am truly astonished that such a complex and responsible job could be assigned to a man who had just joined the company, had no previous experience of the industry and had no legal qualification. However, I tackled the job with huge enthusiasm and did not feel in awe of its magnitude or have any serious doubts about my ability to produce a competently written draft contract for negotiation.

In June 1966, I travelled with Eric Jenkins to St. Louis, Missouri, my first visit to the United States, which in itself was exciting for me. The government was buying for the RAF Phantom fighters built by MacDonnell in St. Louis and the Ministry of Defence had called on HSA to take care of major maintenance of these fighters in the United Kingdom once they were delivered. For this purpose we needed to have a licence agreement with MacDonnell whereby they would licence to HSA patents and technical know-how, which we would need for the purpose. This was a baptism of fire for me. Intellectual property* licences between companies on such lines are part of the lifeblood of industry and a regular occupation of lawyers employed in industry. It fell to me to draft a suitable agreement to take with us to form the basis of our negotiations. I had never written anything of the kind

*Intellectual property – an expression covering patents for inventions, trademarks, copyright in documents and drawings, registered designs and technical know-how related to particular industrial products or processes. The exclusive ownership and use of such rights are of crucial importance to companies in manufacturing and service industries, which will go to great lengths to protect them against others who may seek to engage in unlawful copying or otherwise infringe the rights to the detriment of the owners. Agreements whereby one company allows another company to use particular intellectual property rights, usually against payment of royalties, are known as licence agreements.

before so I started off by buying abook containing precedents for intellectual property agreements to give me some basic guidance. I drafted an agreement on as professional a basis as I could manage which Eric Jenkins examined and accepted before we left. In retrospect, it is truly astonishing that my draft, obviously with some changes resulting from our negotiations with the MacDonnell managers responsible, was accepted and resulted in a signed agreement which put HSA into the position it needed to be in to take on its responsibilities to the RAF. The agreement was expressed to last fifteen years and I know that in fact it lasted longer.

An interesting feature of the negotiations was that MacDonnell's team was made up of tough and experienced managers who were assisted by one lawyer who frankly was not very competent. On the surface, it was an unequal contest between a professionally qualified American in house lawyer on the staff of a huge company with no doubt several other lawyers, and myself, an unqualified legal assistant with a law degree and a certain amount of miscellaneous legal experience. In the event my opposite number contributed little to the discussion or the drafting and was unable to answer a few simple questions which I asked him about the laws of New York which were to govern the contract.

By now, three months after joining HSA, I had decided that I must do something about becoming professionally qualified, so with encouragement from Eric Jenkins I joined Gray's Inn as a student and with the aid of correspondence courses began to work for the Bar examinations in my spare time. It was hard going but I had a tremendous amount of support from Megan, and in the summer of 1968 at the age of 37, I was called to the Bar in Gray's Inn hall. The law had long been my mistress and now I had married her.

HSA had been formed two years before I joined by a merger of several aircraft manufacturing companies with such famous names as Hawker Aircraft, De Havilland, Blackburn and A.V.

Roe. The huge expansion of the industry during the war had left far more companies in being than could expect to continue separately in peace time when obviously the government's spending on military aircraft would be greatly reduced, so eventually, the government, as the industry's biggest customer, pressed them to merge, resulting in two large companies – HSA and British Aircraft Corporation (BAC), which in 1977 were nationalised to form British Aerospace, later privatised and now called BAE Systems. So although I had joined a mature and well established industry, the company and the Head Office which I joined had been only recently formed. It was a very substantial business employing 27,000 people but it had no legal department either at Head Office or at the factories and other establishments scattered around the country. It therefore fell to me, with at first no professional qualification, to set about creating such a department.

I found over the next few years that I was having to advise not just on contract matters in line with my job title. I had to handle problems arising under employment and company law, product liability claims against the company from the United States arising out of injuries and deaths in aircraft accidents, and a wide range of any other legal subjects which were relevant to different aspects of the company's business. I was accepted as the company's legal adviser by managers throughout the company and travelled frequently around the United Kingdom to advise and have discussions with them. I also undertook a lot of international travel, mainly to the United States, Canada, Mexico, France, Germany, Belgium and Egypt, to take part in contract negotiations or deal with any litigation to which the company was a party. The company retained local lawyers in countries in which it did business and I had frequent dealings with them. Like most companies of any international importance, HSA did a great deal of business in the USA, particularly selling its executive jet aircraft, the HS.125. One firm of New York lawyers looked after our commercial business in the USA and a different one, appointed by our insurers, handled the company's defence against product liability claims in the courts of the USA.

Airbus

The most exciting period of my whole career was when I was involved with negotiations in 1969–70 on the European Airbus as HSA's Legal Manager, a title which was conferred on me after I had been called to the Bar. This was a joint venture between French Aérospatiale and Deutsche Airbus, a specially formed consortium of the German aircraft industry, and HSA. The French and German partners were backed by their respective governments, but not so HSA. The United Kingdom did not become a member of what is now the EU until 1 January 1973 and the British government of the day was not enthusiastic about the Airbus project. So HSA, with the backing of its parent company, Hawker Siddeley Group, decided that the venture was worthwhile and invested its own money in it. It proved to be a successful project and now the Airbus consortium is a major competitor with Boeing, supplying its aircraft to the world's airlines. The British contribution was from the start and continues to be the design and manufacture of the wings.

Negotiating on behalf of the company in this project was a task tailor-made for me. By now I had gained a great deal of confidence as an in-house lawyer and set about drafting a contract with the French and German partners which was to form the basis of the company's participation in the project. Aérospatiale was designated as *maître d'oeuvre* for the project and could have insisted on negotiating on the basis of its own draft in French, but in fact we never saw such a draft and everyone was happy to accept mine in English as a starting point. The actual negotiation of this and other contracts dealing with sales and intellectual property related to the project required frequent trips to Paris, sometimes just day trips, and an occasional visit to Hamburg. Some of the sessions took place at HSA's Head Office at Kingston upon Thames or in London. After some time the consortium was joined for part of the work by the Dutch company Fokker, so we had one or two sessions in Amsterdam. I was in my seventh heaven, using French and German frequently and loving the cut and thrust of negotiation. Nowadays, when I occasionally travel on an Airbus I look with quasi-proprietorial pride at the wings.

Concorde

British Aircraft Corporation (BAC) was the British partner with the French industry in the design and manufacture of Concorde as a major joint Anglo-French governmental project. By comparison the airbus, a project not involving British government finance, though the French, German, Dutch and later Spanish governments had financial involvement in it, could well be regarded as a less prestigious affair – the building of a mere subsonic airliner. HSA was not directly involved, but Concorde was a matter of major political and technical importance at the time and clearly of considerable interest to anyone involved in the aircraft industry. There were some signs that the HSA engineers and designers were a trifle jealous of their counterparts in BAC enjoying the excitement of working in a project which stretched the boundaries of engineering technology. Concorde had its first test flight in 1969, so it was very much in the news for much of the time when I was working at HSA. It eventually went into service with Air France and British Airways in January 1976.

In the course of work and socially at lunch and other times, I had much contact with the company's designers and engineers, and in many conversations it became apparent that there was a huge gulf between the way they thought of Concorde and the way the accountants and other commercial staff of the company regarded it. Clearly, the engineers and designers regarded Concorde as the shape of future civil aviation and were impatient of any suggestions that it might be far too expensive to be an economical proposition. There can be no doubt that it was an engineering marvel, able to travel at supersonic speeds at a cruising height of 55,000 feet and more than halve the time taken to cross the Atlantic by subsonic jets. Unfortunately, in economic terms it was a disaster. It had a long gestation period before it eventually flew, with the consequence that it had a narrow fuselage with a maximum capacity of 120 passengers★. By the time it entered service with airlines, the Boeing 747,

★I had the privilege of travelling on Concorde three times on transatlantic flights when I was Company Secretary of Wellcome. I was normally entitled to first-class travel and had become accustomed to the spacious layout of the first-class cabin on the Boeing 747. The wide aisles allowed for the use of trolleys for serving drinks and meals, so for example it was possible for a steward to carve a joint while in flight in similar fashion to a waiter performing the same operation at the Savoy Grill. By contrast, Concorde had a single very narrow aisle, so such luxurious service was not feasible and the stewards had to make do with the same style trolleys as are normally used in economy class. My height is only 5'8" but when I was standing up in the aircraft's toilet my head was up against the ceiling. Concorde had the cramped fuselage of an airliner designed in the 1950s. Clearly, the passengers paid exorbitant fares for travelling at supersonic speeds and enjoyed unlimited champagne and a gourmet menu, but there was otherwise nothing particularly luxurious about travelling on Concorde. However, the speed always generated a certain amount of excitement even among the most sophisticated passengers. On a bulkhead at the front of the passenger cabin there was an indicator which told us when the aircraft reached Mach 1 and was flying supersonically. When the indicator showed that magic figure the passengers usually cheered.

a wide-bodied passenger aircraft capable of carrying 400 or more passengers, was already well established, having entered service in 1971. The very costly Anglo-French development programme coupled with the low carrying capacity meant that the operating costs in airline service were prohibitive. The fact that passengers could be charged a much higher fare for the benefit of supersonic travel than normal first class fare on subsonic aircraft did not come anywhere near compensating for this. Another disadvantage of the aircraft was the boom which it created when travelling at supersonic speeds, which barred it in practice from travelling at such speed over built-up areas. This limited Concorde's use to transatlantic flights from London or Paris to New York, Washington or other cities on the US eastern seaboard. The aircraft's engines guzzled vast quantities of aviation fuel, which imposed a similar restraint on range.

Concorde was bought by only two airlines, Air France and British Airways, both at the time nationally owned by governments whose taxpayers had financed the development costs. In contemporary figures, those costs were around £1.3 billion, which might now be equivalent to £8 billion. Only twenty aircraft were sold, so the overall loss was huge. The fact that there were so few sales meant that the cost of spares supplied by the manufacturers when the aircraft were in service added to the very high operating costs, led to decisions by both airlines to withdraw the aircraft from service in 2003. An Air France Concorde had crashed on takeoff from Paris in July 2000, the crash being caused by a piece of metal debris left behind on the runway by another plane, which punctured Concorde's tyres. This led to Concorde being grounded for some time. After some modifications, flights were resumed by the two airlines in November 2001, but by then the fortunes of airlines generally had been adversely affected by the concerns of passengers after 9/11.

It was difficult to persuade engineers and designers to accept that financial and commercial factors were an unavoidable constraint on the development of aviation. To a large extent they had often been shielded from harsh economic realities by working on programmes which were financed from public funds, particularly for the development of military aircraft. The Concorde programme had provided a similarly protected environment for the development of a prestigious civil airliner, but one which sadly never came anywhere near the ambitions of the two governments and the two companies involved to conquer the world's civil aviation market.

Rolls Royce

The collapse of Rolls Royce, Britain's main manufacturer of aero engines, in February 1971, was an object lesson in the disasters which can occur if engineers are allowed to dominate the fortunes of a high-tech company and override the wishes of prudent accountants. The company had entered into a contract with Lockheed, the American aircraft manufacturer, for the development and supply of a new type of jet engine, the RB211, one revolutionary feature of which was the use of carbon fibre for the fan blades. At the time when the contract was signed development of the RB211 was still under way but the company nevertheless, in spite of all the unknown factors which can affect the costings of such an advanced and complex project, committed itself to supplying the engines to Lockheed at a fixed price. Disaster struck when the board of Rolls Royce realised that they could no longer pay the company's debts as they became due and therefore had to cease trading. A date which I can never forget is 4 February 1971, the date on which a receiver was appointed by the banks. Under company law at that time a receiver took over from the board of directors sole authority to manage the company's affairs. The receiver on this occasion was Rupert Nicholson, senior partner in one of Britain's main accountancy firms, who moved in to the offices of Rolls Royce with a large team of accountants.

This was a catastrophe, not only for Rolls Royce, but also for the nation's aerial defences and for HSA , as all the RAF's aircraft and all aircraft then in production or development by HAS were powered by Rolls Royce engines. Critical action was needed by the government and an urgent meeting was convened on a Sunday by the then Prime Minister, Ted Heath, with cabinet ministers and senior representatives of the company. The decision was taken that the company's assets must be taken into national ownership and an emergency Bill was tabled in Parliament to achieve this. A new company, Rolls Royce (1971) Limited was formed, 100% owned by the government, which bought all the assets from the receiver with public money. This was an ironic step for a Conservative government to have to take, but in the circumstances unavoidable.

This was a clear case in which a company engaged in advanced technological projects – the development and manufacture of jet engines for civil and military aircraft – had allowed the engineers to take charge and to pursue those projects without regard for proper financial constraints. Matters had reached the stage at which the board had to stop trading or the directors would have been risking prosecution for the offence of fraudulent trading. These events received plenty of publicity at the time, but in spite of all the evidence of mismanagement I still found in my casual conversations with engineers employed by HSA, an unwillingness to accept the facts. Several times I heard it suggested that there had been no need for Rolls Royce to cease trading and that the company was being victimised. I tried several times to explain that the company had reached a point at which it would no longer be able to pay its wages and other bills at the end of the month, but my colleagues had difficulty accepting this.

The result of the takeover by the receiver of the assets of Rolls Royce was that he had to make it his priority to sell off the assets so as to pay off the debts owed by the company to the banks which had appointed him. He was able to disclaim any contractual obligations with third parties which he considered onerous, and this was the case with several of the major contracts between HSA and RR. In consequence HSA was able to claim damages for breach of contract. Early meetings were required between lawyers and contract negotiators on both sides, and I had to travel to RR's Head Office in Derby at the end of February 1971 for this purpose. By now the legislation to take over the assets was going through Parliament and normal work was continuing in RR's factories and offices. I found it remarkable that in spite of the company's insolvency there were no signs of what one would have thought to be a necessary belt tightening. A car driven by a uniformed chauffeur met me at Derby Station and drove me to the offices. Some men were mowing the lawns and others were cleaning the windows. I was at meetings for several hours, but we had a break for a good lunch with all the trimmings, such as napkins and waitress service, which were normal on such occasions in the offices of leading companies.

The Trident Crash Inquiry

On 18 June 1972, a Trident aircraft of British European Airways* (BEA), shortly after taking off from Heathrow on a flight to Brussels, crashed near Staines. The crew of six and 112 passengers were all killed. It crashed in open fields, though close to buildings, and there were no casualties to people on the ground or damage to buildings. Sir Geoffrey Lane, at that time a High Court judge and later Lord Chief Justice, was appointed to be the Commissioner of the Inquiry which was ordered by the Lord Chancellor. He was assisted by Sir Morien Morgan, a distinguished engineer and Captain J W Jessup, an experienced

*At this time there were two nationalised airlines, British Overseas Airways Corporation and British European Airways, which were later privatised and merged to form the present British Airways.

airline pilot. HSA as designer and manufacturer of the Trident was required to give evidence at the Inquiry, which began on 20 November 1972, and continued with breaks until 25 January 1973. Other parties attending the Inquiry included BEA, the Air Accidents Investigation Branch and the Civil Aviation Authority. The Inquiry was held at the Piccadilly Hotel in London.

We appointed Peter Webster QC – later a High Court judge – with Anthony Barraclough – who later became Parliamentary Ombudsman – as his junior to represent the company at the Inquiry. This was a major event for the company and I was present most of the time as the company's legal manager, but very much in a supporting role. The evidence given by the company covered many matters relevant to the Inquiry and senior staff from the company's establishment at Hatfield, where the Trident was manufactured, attended the sessions of the Inquiry. The names I recall among the staff who attended are John Wilson, an experienced pilot, Charles Caliendi, a senior design engineer, and John Cunningham, the company's senior test pilot. He had become famous during the war as Group Captain Cunningham and after the war was senior test pilot for de Havilland, one of HSA's predecessor companies. We hired a suite at the hotel for the duration of the Inquiry and held meetings there at the end of each day's proceedings. The Inquiry was a major public event and of much importance to the company, which is reflected by the fact that our daily sessions were frequently attended by Jim Thorne, one of the directors and General Manager at Hatfield, and from time to time the company's Chairman, Sir Arnold Hall, came as a member of the public to listen to the Inquiry. Most of the evidence from the company was highly technical, dealing with the aircraft's flight control systems, aerodynamics and other recondite subjects.

A curious feature of the proceedings was that two or three American lawyers sought and were granted leave to appear at the Inquiry, which gave them the right to receive all copies of papers submitted in evidence and to cross-examine witnesses who gave oral evidence. The justification for their requesting leave to appear was that there were some Americans among the deceased passengers and they were appointed to represent the families of those passengers in litigation which could be expected to follow the publication of the Inquiry's findings. We had no reason to object to their being given leave, but I became incensed in the course of the Inquiry when I discovered that one of the American lawyers was using the experiences of his appearance to write articles in a New York legal periodical, clearly a means of advertising himself in a way which at the time would have been treated as an act of serious professional misconduct on the part of any British solicitor or barrister. I was unable to persuade our counsel to raise objections to this with Sir Geoffrey Lane. I was appalled when this same American lawyer was allowed to address the Inquiry making submissions before all the evidence had been heard, simply because he had a case in New York and needed to leave early – an indulgence which would certainly not have been allowed to British lawyers.

The Inquiry undertook an exhaustive and painstaking investigation of the accident and produced a detailed and comprehensive report. The Trident somewhat unusually was designed to be operated by three pilots, in this case an experienced captain and two relatively junior pilots whose training was found to have been defective in a number of fatal respects. The event which appears to have started the tragedy was that the captain had a heart attack shortly after takeoff. At this time aircraft were not fitted with cockpit voice recorders, so there is no record of exchanges between the other pilots which could have helped to explain why they took actions in response to the captain's condition which were irrational and fatal. One of the recommendations of the Inquiry was that cockpit voice recorders should be a mandatory requirement for civil transport aircraft. However, the readings from the Trident's flight data recorder, colloquially known as the 'black box', were a central part of the evidence and gave the Inquiry precise details of speed, height, movements of control surfaces and other vital information which enabled it to say with accuracy exactly what happened, but could not explain why such an irrational train of events took place and resulted in a major tragedy. For this purpose the Inquiry had to rely on a great deal of evidence on different aspects of the accident, such as medical reports, records of the training of the two junior pilots and evidence given by HSA's witnesses on the design and performance of the Trident.

The Inquiry concluded that the captain's abnormal heart condition had led to a lack of concentration and impaired judgement which would account for the aircraft flying at too low a speed. This error ought to have been noticed by one of the other pilots whose task was to monitor the instruments, but it is likely that both other pilots were distracted by the captain's illness. The second serious error was that the leading edge droop was retracted at much too low a speed. On takeoff an aircraft needs to have maximum wing lift and the Trident was designed with both leading edge and trailing edge flaps which had to be extended and remain extended until the correct speed was reached after takeoff. Because of this second error the aircraft began to stall.

It should be appreciated that the Trident had all three engines mounted in the tail assembly. A plane with engines mounted on the wings would tend to go nose first into a stall and in doing so gain speed which could enable it to come out of the stall. But the weight of the engines in the tail meant that if the Trident stalled it would go tail first. To compensate for this the aircraft was fitted with a stick-push system which automatically operated to push the nose down at the outset of a stall. The system operated as intended and would be accompanied by a loud klaxon in the cockpit to warn the crew that the aircraft was stalling and there was a need to take action to recover. However, the reaction of the two pilots to the warning was to assume that the stick push was malfunctioning and to operate a lever which dumped the stall recovery system and caused the leading edge flap to be retracted. As a result the aircraft went into an irrecoverable stall and crashed.

The Trident crash resulted in claims against the airline, particularly on behalf of the families of the deceased American passengers, whose counsel had been allowed to address the Inquiry. There may also have been claims in the United Kingdom courts though I do not recall any and certainly there were none against HSA in the United Kingdom, though there were some in the USA. I left the company in November 1976, and to the best of my recollection the American cases against the company arising out of the Trident crash had not been concluded. The Inquiry Report lists twelve factors as causing the crash – the captain's heart attack and ten others which may be summarised as pilot error, four of which are listed as failures in training of pilots. The only cause which could be said to put part of the blame on HSA as designer and manufacturer of the Trident is the final one: 'Lack of any mechanism to prevent retraction of the droops at too low a speed after flap-retraction.' This was a little unfair, as the retraction of the droops at sixty knots below proper speed, thus causing the aircraft to enter a stall regime, was contrary to the instructions in the aircraft's Flight Manual and therefore clearly attributable to a failure in training and pilot error. As explained above, when the aircraft entered the stall regime the stick push immediately operated to pull the plane out of the stall and a klaxon sounded as a warning of the stall. The crew had ample opportunity to prevent the accident but failed to take advantage of it, probably because of a combination of panic brought about by the captain's heart attack and lack of experience and/or training.

BACFI

Soon after I was called to the Bar, I joined the Bar Association for Commerce Finance and Industry – BACFI. The Association was formed in 1965 to represent the interests of barristers employed as legal advisers to manufacturing and service companies, banks and others, and is still going strong. The important function of BACFI has always been to promote the proper professional standing of its members. The Bar Council always looked down on employed barristers as barristers in name only and it took some years before BACFI was able to clear the first hurdle of abolishing the rule that counsel must be instructed by a solicitor, which used to have the consequence that a senior barrister working in a company's legal department would have to call upon a solicitor colleague who might be very junior to him to sign on the company's behalf instructions to independent counsel to advise on a particular matter or to act in litigation on the company's behalf.

From the beginning of joining BACFI, I became actively involved in its affairs. For some years I was chairman of its Law Reform Committee, an onerous but enjoyable responsibility. It fell to us to consider proposals on reform of different aspects of the law which had a bearing on the businesses of our various employers and in appropriate cases to write and submit our views to the bodies concerned. The proposals came from a variety of sources, the Law Commission, various government departments such as the Department of Employment on employment laws, the EU or even the United Nations. Often we were commenting on legislation such as the Industrial Relations Bill introduced by Ted Heath's government when it was going through Parliament.

Crossing Swords with Lord Hailsham

BACFI has always had an annual dinner and other regular functions such as are normally held by associations of this kind. In October 1983, we had our dinner in the Hall of the Middle Temple with over 100 members of BACFI and their spouses present, and the guest of honour was the then Lord Chancellor, the late Lord Hailsham. The custom always was that the guest of honour should be asked to propose the toast of BACFI. Lord Hailsham embarked on a speech concentrating on what he described in explicit terms as BACFI's failure to respond to law reform proposals on various commercial subjects which had been made by his department and by the Law Commission. His speech was decidedly short on diplomacy and elementary politeness; he was after all enjoying our hospitality. Furthermore, we had had no warning of his highly critical remarks. I was junior Vice-Chairman of BACFI at the time, meaning that I was designated as the next Chairman taking over in the following year. It fell to me in accordance with custom to respond and thank the guest of honour. I had prepared a few appropriate complimentary remarks but decided on the spot to put them aside and embarked on an impromptu response, telling the Lord Chancellor that he had seriously misjudged us. I referred to my recent experience as Chairman of the Law Reform, a position which I had held for five years, and pointed out that we had to do our best to deal with law reform proposals coming to us from many sources and not just from the Lord Chancellor's Department or the Law Commission. I added that the proposals which we had to consider for the most part would have been drafted by British, European, or other international civil servants or lawyers for whom this would be part of their full time paid employment, whereas our efforts were undertaken in our unpaid spare time – a most unequal contest. It was apparent to me that the Lord Chancellor had been badly briefed by his civil servants when considering what he should say in his speech. They had failed to make him aware and may well have been deplorably unaware themselves of the many sources of law reform with which we had to contend. Hailsham was a prominent member of the government of the day and famous as a lawyer and politician and a prime minister manqué – the Boris Johnson of his day – so it was audacious on my part as a humble employed barrister to respond in this way, but I felt that he deserved the treatment. After dinner Hailsham was looking slightly chastened by this public rebuff. I spoke to him briefly and made it clear that while I had no cause to regret or apologise for what I had said I was sorry for the necessity to say it.

Later that month, with the agreement of the then Chairman and other committee members of BACFI, I wrote a long letter to Hailsham, setting out in detail the main tasks in areas of law which were relevant to the businesses of our employers which we had undertaken in recent years. Thirty-one years later the list is still a most impressive inventory of the amount of work we did. A week later I received a three-page letter from Hailsham in which he expressed the hope that we had not taken any offence at his remarks, since nothing was further from his thoughts. He accepted the force of the points I had made in my speech which I had enlarged on in my letter. His final paragraph is worth quoting:

"I intended to do no more than encourage you to submit observations," [i.e. on law reform proposals] "because while the comments of practising lawyers and academics are useful, in the end the best judges of the law are perhaps *those who have to apply it to their everyday work*" [emphasis supplied], "and for that reason the comments of BACFI on whether reform of the law is needed, and if so what form it should take, are particularly appreciated."

The fact that Hailsham replied at length and so promptly could reasonably be taken as an indication that he understood that he had committed a gaffe and realised that he had to make amends. Looking at that final paragraph now, it becomes apparent that Hailsham made a distinction between members of BACFI, identified by the italicised words and 'practising lawyers', by whom he obviously meant lawyers in independent practice, whether solicitors or barristers. By implication, in spite of his emollient words, it is clear that he did not regard BACFI members as practising lawyers, in spite of their being barristers and being employed full time on legal work. The sting was in the tail. In 1983 we had not yet achieved the important objective of having the constitution of the Bar revised to make it clear that barristers in employment providing professional services to their employers were just as much in practice as those working in the courts or in chambers. That came later.

Lord Denning and Others

Every year BACFI holds an annual event called the Denning Lecture, after perhaps the most distinguished English judge of the mid-twentieth century. He had been a hero of ours, a radical and revolutionary judge when I was a law student at Cambridge, having achieved fame if not notoriety by a revolutionary judgement in the case of *High Trees* [1947] KB 130 on the basic law of contract. When I was Chairman of BACFI he was Master of the Rolls, head of the Court of Appeal. He was happy to allow us to name this annual lecture after him. BACFI also holds an annual dinner. It fell to me to preside over both these events in 1984. At that time I was Company Secretary of Wellcome, with its Head Office in the Wellcome Building across the road from Euston Station. I took full advantage of the prestigious facilities which the building offered to organise in the directors' dining room a dinner for the speaker, Lord Justice Parker, Lord Denning, the BACFI President Lord Tempelmann, Bob Alexander QC, then Vice Chairman of the Bar Council, and other leading lights of the Bar and judiciary, with wives. I arranged the annual dinner of BACFI in the Institute of Directors, across from the Athaeneum, and invited the late Sir David Steele, former Chairman of BP and at that time Chairman of the Wellcome Trust, as guest of honour. Sir David started off as a solicitor working for BP so the world of employed lawyers was familiar to him. My immediate neighbour at the table at the time was the then Attorney General, Sir Michael Havers, later briefly Lord Havers, Lord Chancellor for just a few months before his death. This was in the middle of the miners' strike and Havers confidentially told me of the various unsuccessful attempts by members of the government of the day to find some sort of evidence which could be used to discredit publicly Arthur Scargill, the firebrand leader of the Miners' Union, as a means of bringing the strike to an end.

Bob Alexander was a prominent and distinguished member of the Bar who was born in 1936 and died in 2005. When I was chairman of BACFI, I was invited to sit as a member of a Bar disciplinary tribunal which had to deal with the case of an employed barrister who was charged with an offence against the Bar's Code of Conduct. The barrister appeared accompanied by Bob Alexander as his counsel and in effect pleaded guilty. Bob put in an eloquent plea of mitigation on his client's behalf, and we let the man off with a formal reprimand.

Bob was Chairman of the Bar Council from 1985 to 1986 and part of his time in that office coincided with the last six months of my term as BACFI Chairman, which meant that we had dealings with each other on matters of interest to the profession generally. He was a most genial person to deal with, treated me as an equal, and did not show any of the unwarranted and supercilious superiority over employed barristers which at the time was an all too common attitude on the part of those in independent practice. We met frequently at Bar Council gatherings and were on first-name terms. One year he delivered the Denning Lecture on the subject of the City Panel on Takeovers and Mergers, of which he was Chairman. In the case for which he is best remembered he represented Lord Archer in the latter's libel action against the *Daily Star* in 1987. It is sad to have to recall that it was later shown that Archer had won on the basis of seriously perjured evidence, which resulted in his going to jail. Bob was ennobled as Lord Alexander of Weedon in 1988, and retired from practice in 1989, on taking up an appointment as Chairman of National Westminster Bank. In early 2006, following his death, a memorial service was held in St Margaret's Westminster, which I attended. Bob had been Chancellor of Exeter University among other prominent appointments and the address was given by the Vice-Chancellor. There was a reception after the service in Whitehall Palace, attended by many distinguished people. I overheard a conversation in which Sir John Major said that if he had won the 1997 General Election he would have invited Bob to become Lord Chancellor.

Taking Silk

By the 1980s I was established as having been Company Secretary of Wellcome (a major company and a multinational in the pharmaceutical industry) since 1976, was active as a BACFI committee member and had been chairman from 1984 to 1985. This meant that I had achieved modest eminence and provided me with a basis to justify submitting an application to be appointed as one of Her Majesty's Counsel. There were already six employed barristers who had been thus appointed, one of the most recent being the late James Keir, for some years Company Secretary of Unilever and a former Chairman of BACFI, who was a good friend and encouraged me in this endeavour. I applied I think in four consecutive years and was rejected each time. In 1987, I had concluded that it was pointless to submit another application, but Megan insisted that I must try again. I filled in the form and secured the support of my boss, chairman and chief executive of Wellcome, the late Sir Alfred Shepperd, and of Lord Tempelmann, who had been a most supportive President of BACFI when I was Chairman. Forms had to be submitted by noon on a particular date, and I had left it so late that I had to take a taxi to the House of Lords that morning to make sure that I got the application in on time.

It was a joy when the letter came telling me that I had been appointed. The system now is different but at that time the responsibility for appointments rested with the Lord Chancellor. This meant that in 1983, when I had my public disagreement with the then Lord Chancellor, Lord Hailsham, I already had at least one unsuccessful application behind me. When I took the decision on my feet to go ahead and publicly correct the Lord Chancellor's deplorable misapprehensions about BACFI, it certainly crossed my mind that in doing so I might be making an enemy and excluding myself for ever from any possibility of obtaining the desired appointment, though that did not deter me. Hailsham was still Lord Chancellor in 1987, and if he recalled the earlier exchanges between us clearly did not hold them against me.

The custom was and possibly still is to invite all newly appointed silks for the year to a ceremony at the House of Lords at which each in turn had to stand and take a form of oath of office. This involved putting on the full regalia of Queen's Counsel, much more elaborate and even more archaic than the robes worn by Queen's Counsel in court – silk gown, full bottomed wig, fancy jacket and waistcoat, bands, white silk gloves, knee breeches, black tights and buckled shoes. I had to hire the lot from outfitters Ede and Ravenscroft in Chancery Lane and go there on the morning of the ceremony to be dressed. This involved my stripping down to underpants and vest and having two of the staff of Ede and Ravenscroft put on me items of clothing which I would have been incapable of putting on myself unaided. It is a ridiculously out-of-date outfit which was long obsolete at the time when Victoria came to the throne. Some cautious steps have been taken by the Bar towards modernising court dress by abandoning wigs in the civil courts, but wigs are still regarded as an essential concomitant to the dispensation of justice in the Crown Courts. It is typically anomalous that justices of the Supreme Court, the highest court in the land, do not wear wigs or gowns but go to work in normal suits, though counsel who appear before them still have to be properly robed.

Another requirement of the ceremony was that I had to be accompanied by my clerk. As I was not in independent practice and never had a seat in chambers, I did not have a clerk but was able through the good offices of a fellow member of BACFI to arrange to borrow a barrister's clerk for the day. He had to hire morning dress, for which I reimbursed him, and I also gave him £100 for his trouble. My secretary Irene Lawson would have been delighted to take on the role, but she would have been quite lost among the milling crowd of barristers in fancy dress and their clerks in the splendid but to her unfamiliar surroundings of the House of Lords. I was able to use the chairman's Bentley and driver for the day to take myself and family first to Chancery Lane, then to the House of Lords and afterwards to Gray's Inn for lunch. Afterwards we all went to the Law Courts where the final part of the day's ceremonies required all new QCs to present themselves in each Division of the High Court and the Court of Appeal.

I was the seventh and last full QC to be appointed from the membership of BACFI. Since 1987, one or two BACFI members have been appointed as Honorary QCs, not quite the same thing. Taking silk for a barrister in private practice means an obvious increase in status and seniority and the ability to charge higher fees. In my case it did not mean any rise in salary, but my appointment was recorded in Wellcome's house journal and as Company Secretary I was able to record in the Board Minutes the Board's congratulations. My name always appeared in the company's published report and accounts so from then on the letters QC appeared after it.

My years as a member of the Committee of BACFI, and especially when I was Chairman or holder of another office, were stimulating and enjoyable. For much of the time I served as BACFI representative on the Bar Council and on committees of the Bar Council, dealing with law reform and other subjects. I was at the same time doing a full time very senior job as Company Secretary of Wellcome, fitting in these professional activities mostly in the evenings. It all meant long hours and a packed and busy schedule. It also meant less time at home and I owe a debt of gratitude to my wife Megan for her support and encouragement in those years.

The Wellcome Foundation Limited – Company Secretary

The position of Company Secretary of Wellcome was the most senior appointment for which I was ever considered. The logic for my moving on from an appointment with HSA which I enjoyed enormously was the looming prospect of nationalisation of the aircraft industry. The Bill for this began its passage through Parliament in 1975 and nationalisation occurred in 1977, by which time I had already moved on. The intended consequence of the Bill was that the two main companies, Hawker Siddeley Aviation and British Aircraft Corporation, would be merged on nationalisation to form British Aerospace. Mergers inevitably result in some redundancies and in this case I felt that I might well be a casualty, as my opposite number in BAC was on the company's board of directors and I, though I now had the courtesy title of Executive Director Legal, did not have a corresponding status in HSA. (Nationalisation is the subject of a separate chapter.)

This was a move to a much bigger job with greater responsibilities and a big increase in pay, from about £10,000 to £15,000 a year – a high salary in 1976. At HSA, I had had just two people working for me: a lawyer as my assistant and a secretary. Now I was in charge of four departments: legal, trademarks, insurance, and an Assistant Secretary who also looked after Regulatory Control, the specialised and detailed legal regime governing the development, licensing, manufacture, sale and advertising of medicines to which companies in the pharmaceutical industry are subject. I had a staff of sixty mainly professional and administrative staff and an annual budget which after a few years reached £13 million. In addition I had the normal responsibilities of a Company Secretary attending all Board meetings, keeping the minutes and carrying out other formal duties. This should have been an exciting prospect, but when I was first offered the job I turned it down after much pondering. I just had the feeling that I would not be happy in the job. The chairman at the time, Alfred Shepperd, called me in and persuaded me to change my mind. I started work in November 1976, and soon realised that my earlier apprehensions had been well founded. For a long time I was most unhappy and regretted the move I had made. These were the reasons:

- I missed the variety and freedom which I had had as legal adviser to HSA.
- The management responsibilities combined with the formal tasks of a Company Secretary meant a much more circumscribed daily routine. The work from day to day in my early days there was much less enjoyable.
- My predecessor had been a sick man for the past two years and had not exercised much control over the senior managers reporting to him. This meant that they had been accustomed to working without that control and to a large extent reporting to the Chairman and Chief Executive direct instead of to him. It took a long time for me to change this and assert my authority.
- I had the difficulty inevitably faced by someone moving from a senior post in industry to an even more senior post in an unrelated industry, of having to become familiar with a complex and very different environment from what I had known before.

HSA was a substantial company manufacturing aircraft in the UK though selling its products worldwide. Wellcome was also a big company, but very much a multinational with its main base for research and development and manufacturing in the UK, but with a substantial subsidiary in the United States, also engaged in research, development and manufacturing. The nature of its business necessitated the establishment of subsidiary companies or branches in most major countries and many lesser ones, e.g. France, Germany, Spain, Italy, Ireland, Brazil, Mexico, Canada, Japan, India, Pakistan, Hong Kong, Singapore, Australia, New Zealand, Nigeria, Kenya and South Africa. In some countries restrictions on imports of pharmaceutical products or other legislation made it necessary to set up factories to meet the needs of the local market.

After a few unhappy months I grabbed the opportunity of making my working life much more enjoyable. The company had a need to establish a new partnership for the management and expansion of its business in Japan, at that time the world's third largest market after the USA and the EU, though now far eclipsed by China. I had myself made a member of the management team set up for this purpose and set about drafting the necessary agreements. In 1977, I travelled to Japan with the rest of the team four times and had the satisfaction of taking an important part of the credit for establishing a new partnership for the management of our Japanese business with the pharmaceutical arm of Sumitomo, one of the Japanese zaibatsu. Wellcome had its own trading subsidiary in Japan, Nippon Wellcome, of which I became a director, and I continued to pay regular visits to Japan for the rest of my time with Wellcome. I enjoyed the stimulus of negotiating with the managers of Sumitomo, for whom I acquired the greatest respect. I did not have much opportunity for sightseeing, but I was able to sample the pleasures of travelling on Japan's high speed trains, the shinkansen, and acquired a taste for the delicacies of Japanese cuisine.

I also later became a director of subsidiary companies in India, Pakistan and Nigeria, which involved travelling to these countries for Board meetings. My earlier experiences in Sierra Leone and India made it a congenial task to accustom myself to the environment of these subsidiaries which were and are members of the Commonwealth. Of course, my main responsibilities as Company Secretary tied me very much to the routines of Head

Office, Board meetings and commuting. Whatever international travel I did on Wellcome's account had to be fitted in with these duties. I found that my boss, Alfred Shepperd, positively encouraged my involvement in the company's international business and did not discourage me from travelling.

From 1981, until my retirement from Wellcome in 1992, the Board in most years held a strategic meeting at which it was joined by the most senior managers from around the world. For this purpose I travelled with the Board to the United States, France, Germany, Italy, Spain, Singapore and Australia. For three of those years we took over a medium-sized hotel in Bermuda, the Glencoe at Salt Kettle, and finally came home to the luxury hotel Chewton Glen near Bournemouth.

The Flotation of Wellcome

The big event of my years at Wellcome was the company's flotation on the London Stock Exchange. I need to explain the unique nature of Wellcome and its origins. The business was founded in 1880 by Henry Wellcome, an American who became naturalised and was knighted. His only child was a son who was mentally defective, so Wellcome left a small legacy enabling a trust fund to be established for his son's maintenance for the rest of his life.*Apart from this and a few other legacies, he left

* The son's name was Mounteney Wellcome and the amount settled on him was £10,000, a substantial sum in 1936, but a relatively insignificant portion of Sir Henry Wellcome's huge wealth. One of my duties as Company Secretary was to act as Mounteney's trustee, along with another trustee appointed by the Wellcome Trust. Mounteney and his wife Jean lived in a house at Stony Stratford, near Milton Keynes, and I visited them there from time to time. Jean was a member of a local family who owned her own farm. She and Mounteney were married in their forties and did not have any children.

the whole of his estate, including the substantial company he had created, to a trust – the Wellcome Trust – established in 1936 by his will when he died. The company was given the confusing name The Wellcome Foundation Limited, and all its share capital was owned by the Wellcome Trust, now one of the world's most prosperous charities and a major funder of scientific and medical research. In 1976, I thus became Company Secretary to what was Britain's biggest privately owned company. I soon learned to cope with the unavoidable confusion which the similarity of these two names created. Members of the public naturally assumed that the name 'Foundation' connoted a charitable body and I had many calls from doctors and others seeking grants to fund particular research projects. I normally gave them the Trust's telephone number. It was perhaps not entirely surprising that even some of the company's employees, especially research scientists, were under the mistaken impression that they were working for a charity rather than for a company which was wholly owned by a charity*.

Dividends from the company were the Wellcome Trust's main source of income. The Annual General Meeting (AGM) was a meeting between the members of the Board and the trustees. These were distinguished scientists for the most part, chaired when I first joined by the late Lord Franks, former British ambassador to Washington and holder of numerous other

* Even that august intellectual organ *The Times* had a problem in differentiating the company and the Trust. When our chairman Sir Alfred Shepperd died the headline of his full page obituary on 20 October 2007 referred to him in large capitals as 'Chief Executive of the Wellcome Trust'. The body of the obituary contained several other serious errors. I sent off a letter promptly to the editor pointing out all these mistakes and was pleased that it was published in full on the obituary pages. Such a howler would have merited a public apology, but none was forthcoming.

senior establishment appointments. Lord Franks was succeeded in the early 1980s by Sir David Steele, former Chairman of BP, who early on became concerned that the Trust, to use his own expression, had all its eggs in one basket. Even though he acknowledged that it was a basket of very high quality, he was concerned at the detrimental effect on the Trust of any possible serious downturn in the company's fortunes. The result of his concerns was a decision by the Trustees that the company must become a public limited company listed on the London Stock Exchange and to achieve this the Trust would offer 26% of its shares to the public. This intention was communicated to the Board at its meeting in April 1985, and from that point on the process of preparing the company for flotation began.

This meant a huge amount of work for many of us over the rest of 1985, and the early months of 1986, and particularly for the Chairman, Finance Director Martin Brookman, and myself. Flemings, investment bankers acting on behalf of the Wellcome Trust, were in charge of the process and laid down a strict timetable which culminated in the opening of trading in the company's shares on the London Stock Exchange in February 1986. Before that a huge investigation into the affairs of the company known as 'due diligence' had to be undertaken, leading to the preparation and publication of a detailed prospectus on the basis of which shares would be sold to the public. Hordes of lawyers, accountants, stockbrokers and various other denizens of the City descended on Head Office. Access had to be provided to back numbers of Board minutes and other documents. Directors and senior managers had to face detailed inquisitions into the details of the activities for which they were responsible.

After a month or two the first drafts of the prospectus appeared and were circulated each weekend by car (the Internet had not yet been invented) by the printers to the privileged few including myself who had to read them before Monday morning and make comments or corrections. Business connected with flotation dominated every Board meeting and we had to have present at these meetings the company's external lawyers, auditors and investment bankers. Preparations were made for company and group employees around the world to be given a preferential allocation of shares at the opening of dealings and for them to be able to participate in share options at favourable prices which would become exercisable three years after flotation.

In common with other members of my staff I had to put in long hours including weekends. The pressure on me was increased in that the process began halfway through my year of office as Chairman of BACFI, so I had somehow or other to cope as best I could with that extra responsibility. I had to miss taking the chair at just one of BACFI's Committee meetings during 1985.

The issue of Wellcome shares was very popular and was eighteen times oversubscribed. This necessitated a late night meeting at the offices of Flemings at which decisions had to be taken on the basis on which available shares would be issued to a minority of applicants, while the rest would have to be disappointed. As representatives of the company, the Chairman, Finance Director and I could do no more than ensure that there was fair play, as the process of selection involved largely mathematical processes to which we were unable to contribute. The Wellcome public offering of shares was the last to take place on the trading floor of the London Stock Exchange. To mark the occasion all the brokers' stands on the floor were decorated with large logos showing the name WELLCOME and the company trade mark unicorn. After Big Bang on 27 October 1985, all dealings took place via trading screens.

After February 1986, I had to take on the extra responsibilities involved in being Secretary of a public company. It meant having to have regard at all times for the rules of the London Stock Exchange as well the Companies Act. Dealings by any director in the company's shares had to be reported to the LSO and would be made public. I had to keep a record of dealings by senior managers who might be at any time in possession of inside information which could give them an advantage over the public in general in trading in the company's shares. From time to time I had to warn them that they should not deal, usually because the company was about to announce trading results. A public share register had to be maintained, a huge undertaking because from the start we had thousands of shareholders, and I had to identify a suitable firm of registrars to maintain this. I also had to organise the annual general meeting, now a much bigger affair than the previous cosy chats between the directors and the Wellcome Trustees. Notices of the meeting and copies of the Annual Report and Accounts had to be sent out to all shareholders. I had to hire a suitable venue, in the first few years the Great Room at the Grosvenor House Hotel on Park Lane. Secretaries and other staff members were drafted in to act as ushers and the chairman and the rest of the board had to face the shareholders and answer questions about the company's fortunes.

Wellcome was a prominent company in the pharmaceutical industry, with major research establishments in the United Kingdom and United States. Inevitably, some of the work necessitated experiments using live animals, though over the years the need for such experiments has been progressively reduced. This meant that we had to be prepared for hostile demonstrations by animal rights campaigners outside the Grosvenor House Hotel, so we had to make security preparations for the AGM, including contacts with the police. We also had a few shareholders who had bought just one or two shares so that they could attend the meeting and protest from the floor at the company's involvement in animal experiments. There were many other individuals, often retired people of modest means, who bought small numbers of shares so as to have the opportunity of attending AGMs, which they presumably regarded as a form of entertainment which had the advantage of giving them some income in the form of dividends.

Another attraction of AGMs was that major companies with large numbers of shareholders had to hire large venues in hotels and normally provided light refreshments, tea, coffee and cold non-alcoholic drinks for the shareholders. In some cases the shareholders literally made a meal of the occasion and it was not unknown for some of the ladies attending to stuff their handbags with cakes and other goodies to take home. Refreshments might be provided both after and before the meetings, which were usually held in the morning, so the meeting might end at midday or thereabouts. One year my chairman suggested that as our AGM would be ending at almost lunch time it would be more hospitable and appropriate to the hour to offer alcoholic drinks rather than the usual more modest fare. I advised very strongly against this on the ground mainly of cost and also of the problem of coping with and possibly having to eject inebriated shareholders who would be taking full advantage of the availability of free booze. My advice was accepted.

A Royal Visit

The Wellcome Trust was established under the will of Sir Henry Wellcome, who died in 1936. It owned all the shares of The Wellcome Foundation Limited, Britain's biggest private company until its flotation in February 1986. Partly as a result of the company's profitability over many years and partly because of the highly successful flotation, the Trust became, and remains, probably Britain's biggest charity and possibly the world's biggest funder of medical research. It now has a worth of £18 billion and spends £700 million annually on research projects. The Trustees include distinguished scientists and medics. The Trust's wealth and high standing in the scientific world made it appropriate that 1986 should be celebrated as the fiftieth anniversary of its founding. Several important events were organised to mark the anniversary, the most important being a reception at the Trust's headquarters, the Wellcome Building on Euston Road in London. At the time the Wellcome Building was also the company's headquarters, where I worked for thirteen out of my sixteen years as Company Secretary.

This was a major event to which many distinguished guests were invited and the Queen was the guest of honour. The main body of guests assembled in the large boardroom on the mezzanine floor, in which an exhibition displaying the history and scientific activities of the Trust was set up. The Queen and the Duke of Edinburgh arrived and entered the boardroom accompanied by Sir David Steele, Chairman of the Trust and Sir Alfred Shepperd, Chairman and Chief Executive of the company. The Queen signed the visitors' books of the Trust and the company and then started to walk around the boardroom to have a look at the exhibits. Everyone else moved to the sides of the room, leaving a large rectangular space in the middle for the royal couple to walk around. Inevitably, all the guests fell silent and the occasion became acutely embarrassing. After a while the ice was broken by the Duke with one of his notorious quips. He had obviously done his homework and was aware that one of the Wellcome Trust's main activities was funding research into new treatments for diseases, which would often necessitate clinical trials in patients affected by the disease. He spotted a clergyman in the crowd and said in a loud voice, "Ah, nice to see a dog collar. Do you bury their mistakes?" Just the sort of ribald humorous remark that was needed. Everyone became more relaxed and general conversation was resumed.

DAGENHAM AND BOMBAY

Resignation and return to Britain

This is a chapter which in chronological sequence follows on from *Remote Corners*, at the end of which I recorded my decision to resign from the Colonial Service and return to the United Kingdom to take my chances in seeking some sort of employment in a very different field.

I had just passed my 29th birthday. I had a respectable degree from Cambridge, a First in the Modern Languages Tripos Part I and an Upper Second in the Law Tripos Part II, but otherwise no qualifications. I had had after Cambridge a year in London in training for service in Sierra Leone, followed by five years in the colony, all of it spent working in different districts as Assistant District Commissioner, sometimes Acting District Commissioner, combined with the offices of Magistrate and Coroner.

The main reason for my decision to resign was the increasing speed with which the British government was divesting itself of its colonies, particularly in Africa, which inevitably cut short career prospects. (Sierra Leone became independent in April 1961, just sixteen months after my departure.) But there were other reasons. The Colonial Service was not my first choice of career, but one that I had been persuaded to enter after being unsuccessful in my efforts to join the Foreign Service, so from the start I had not felt that it was going to be a lifetime's commitment. Another fact which influenced my decision was that Ghana had already become independent in 1957 and several former administrators from service in the Gold Coast,

Ghana's name as a British colony, having left that service were recruited on short-term contracts as administrative officers for service in Sierra Leone. These men were given seniority on the basis of their past colonial service and blocked any possible path to promotion there might have been for me. The other factor was my age. I was very conscious that the longer I left it to find new employment the more difficult it would be.

The need to make a radical career change after a few years in the Colonial Service obviously affected large numbers of men of my age group who found their prospects cut short by imminent independence. In some cases, older men in particular could opt to remain in the territory in which they were already working and become servants to the government of a newly sovereign state. This would be on the assumption that the new masters were willing to employ them and might carry the risk of facing unequal competition from local indigenous civil servants. A longer term risk, which did in fact materialise for many retired colonial service officers, was to pensions. Another possibility was transfer to another of the remaining colonies, though the pace of granting independence accelerated after 1960, which meant that this was a progressively more and more limited option. For those who could be so fortunate, a transfer to Hong Kong was a happy solution to the problem, as Hong Kong remained a colony until 1997, when it was handed back to China.

What would have been my first choice in the circumstances was to read for the Bar and get myself established in practice. However, although I was a little better off financially than I had been in 1953, when I graduated from Cambridge, I still did not have the wherewithal to finance myself through a period of perhaps two years or more while I took the examinations, ate my dinners at Gray's Inn, found a set of chambers which would accept me as a pupil and started to establish a practice which actually earned some money. I recall that one of my contemporaries from Sierra Leone was fortunate in becoming an articled clerk to a firm of solicitors in the City, but at that time articled clerks, or trainee solicitors as they are now styled, normally had to pay for the privilege of becoming articled and did not earn anything until they had become qualified. So a move into either branch of the legal profession was barred to me on practical financial grounds. The remaining options for mature men seeking to change to a different career varied. Administrative jobs in universities or the BBC were favoured by some. Others became school teachers or were called to holy orders in the Church of England.

So I returned to Britain in November 1959, at the age of 29. I was entitled to a period of paid leave and as I was still a bachelor I was able to collect a refund of contributions which I had paid into the Widows' and Orphans' Pension Fund during my service, a modest £600 or so. I went to stay with my mother at her home in Darwen and began to apply for jobs. The various possibilities which I have described in the previous paragraph either were impractical or did not appeal. I realised that adjusting to a totally new environment would be hard going, but I was still young enough to be ambitious and decided to try to find suitable employment in manufacturing industry, at the time still a much more important feature of the British economy than is the case now in the 21st century.

After a number of interviews with different companies, I was offered a job with Fords at Dagenham and began work there in December 1959. I found lodgings for myself in Goodmayes, part of Ilford, just a short bus journey from the Ford plant at Dagenham.

Joining Ford

Starting work at Fords was a major culture shock for me. Although I had been just an Assistant District Commissioner in Sierra Leone, this gave me some status and dignity. I was a fairly big fish in a small pool, being one of the bosses and having for most of the time a house of my own. Now I became just an insignificant minnow in a very big pool. The Ford estate at Dagenham was, I believe at that time the biggest industrial complex in Europe where many thousands of people were employed and at times around 3000 cars a day came off the assembly lines. It was a vertically integrated manufacturing site, with its own power station, blast furnace, coke ovens and foundry. Most chassis and body parts were made in different factories on the estate and moved around from one site to another by the company's own extensive railway system or by lorries. It had a frontage on the Thames with its own jetty. At one end of the jetty, iron ore was unloaded from ships for the blast furnace, and cars and tractors, either fully built or in crates of parts, would be assembled into complete vehicles in their countries of destination, and loaded onto ships at the other end.

I had been recruited as an Organisation Analyst, an activity falling within the company's personnel division. An organisation the size of Ford, employing thousands of people in complex manufacturing processes, design, sales, accounting and other functions, has a need to keep track of who is responsible for the many different activities. Individuals have to be assigned to particular modest-sized units of management with designated managers. The managers have to know what their responsibilities are and the names and designations of the superior bosses to whom they in their turn have to report. The scope and definition of responsibilities in particular units will often change and there will be frequent changes of names and job titles of individual managers. The section to which I belonged was called Organisation Planning and its function was to monitor and keep track of all these changes, which involved writing up job descriptions of managers and defining the scope of activities of their departments. It was not unusual for there to be conflict between different departments as to who had responsibility for particular functions and it fell to Organisation

Planning to resolve these demarcation disputes. The section had responsibility for producing and keeping up to date the company's Organisation Manual which was a substantial source of reference containing charts in the style of family trees showing the hierarchy of management in all the company's divisions.

This was potentially an interesting and worthwhile job, which the company was prepared to entrust to a small team of graduates with no special technical expertise, including me as a complete newcomer to manufacturing industry but with general management experience in the colonial service. It required broad understanding of how the company worked and how the various functions needed by such a huge and dynamic organisation were allocated to its various divisions. Sorting out organisation statements and drawing organisation charts necessitated much discussion with senior managers. The drawbacks were not so much in the quality or interest of the work as with actual working conditions. I just had to accept being a nobody, paid a modest £900 a year to start with and having to clock on and off daily, the latter being a humiliating comedown after my previous experience. The original Ford Head Office with its frontage on the Thames was no longer able to accommodate all head office staff, and as a result, many were scattered in indiscriminate fashion in small parcels of space in buildings all over the vast Dagenham estate. Organisation Planning had the doubtful privilege of occupying space in the original building, space which amounted to just one office to accommodate all eight of us – a supervisor, four analysts (including me), one secretary and two other junior staff. The office had no natural light, so we were in artificial light all day. In Sierra Leone, I had sometimes had to share an office with one other person, but there was plenty of elbow room and for much of the time I had an office all to myself. I now sometimes found that I had to endure having to share a desk.

Working in such crowded conditions meant that we were much in each other's company and fortunately we all got on well together. I certainly found the company of other graduates of more or less my own age congenial. After I had been there a few months the section was joined by a new recruit, John Southam, a barrister, at the time a little over 30, so a little older than the rest of us. Like so many in the profession he was struggling and after trying for a few years found that he was not able to earn enough to live on, so was happy to find his own salvation in paid employment which was unconnected with the law. We had both come new to industry and new to the particular job at Ford at the same time and I find it instructive in retrospect to compare our respective reactions to the job. I was not enjoying it very much, feeling that I was having to endure a considerable drop in status from being a somebody in Sierra Leone to becoming a nobody in Dagenham. Although the job required a high degree of intelligence and justified the employment of graduates to do it, it did not offer anything comparable to the wide variety and responsibility of being an Assistant District Commissioner. I felt at times like a caged lion. John Southam, by contrast, had exchanged the misery and desperation of trying to make ends meet by his not very successful endeavours at building up a practice in the magistrates' courts and other lowly forums for the security of a regular secure job, with a regular, albeit modest, income and obviously enjoyed it. Some time after I had left the company, in September 1960, he was invited by British Gas, at that time still nationalised, to become their chief in-house legal adviser, a position for which he had previously applied unsuccessfully. He assured me when we met some years later through our mutual membership of the Bar Association for Commerce, Finance and Industry (BACFI) that he had not been actively seeking other employment and was sorry to leave Ford. He was chief legal adviser to British Gas for some years and contributed the chapter on gas supply to the contemporary edition of *Halsbury's Laws of England*. In fact he became another briefless barrister, but achieved that status after a not very successful spell in private practice.

Another adjustment which I found difficult was that of having to find somewhere to live. I found lodgings in a house owned and occupied by an elderly widow in a row of terraced housing in Goodmayes. I had a bed sitting room and the use of a shared bathroom. This was quite a comedown from having a house to myself and employing a cook and a bearer/steward to look after my needs. My landlady made my bed in the morning and prepared breakfast and an evening meal for me. If she thought I was a bit tardy in getting up to go to work she sometimes thumped with her broom on the ceiling below my room. I was usually back in my lodgings by 6pm and became accustomed to my landlady calling upstairs, "It's on the table, Mr Mitchell!" It was not too far to walk to the bus stop from which I could catch a bus to Fords, or as my landlady in her estuary accent called it, "Fowds".

Marriage and India

I have explained in *Remote Corners* that my wife Megan was previously married to Bob Knill, an Agricultural Officer in the colonial service in Sierra Leone, and I first met them both in 1957 at Rokupr, the town on the west side of Sierra Leone where the West African Rice Research Station to which Bob was attached was located, shortly after their daughter Kamini was born in Freetown. Later, they moved to Pujehun on the other side of the country and there sadly in 1959, Bob was killed in a road accident. By this time they had had another child, a son called Howard, and Megan came back with the children as a widow.

I went to see her in her home county of Herefordshire. After a while, I began to visit at weekends and bought a small car second-hand to make the travelling easier. By Easter 1960, we decided to get married. This presented us with a major problem of finding somewhere to live near Dagenham. I did try the alternative of finding a job in Hereford, but was unsuccessful. We had not made any real progress in solving the problem when Megan came up with a brilliant solution. She sent me a cutting from the Situations Vacant pages of *The Daily Telegraph*, advertising a job in India as Company Secretary to a British-owned company at a salary of £3,000 a year – a huge sum to us at that time. I applied for it but without any real expectation of success. I was agreeably surprised to be invited to an interview at the London office of the parent company, Turner & Newall, in Curzon Street. The Personnel Manager, a retired Air Vice Marshal, interviewed me in friendly fashion and before long I was invited to a further interview, this time with the Personnel Manager and with the Managing Director of the Indian Company, Asbestos Cement Limited, who was in Britain on leave. To attend both these interviews I had to get time off from my job at Dagenham and had to resort to telling lies about my reasons for needing it. The second interview was on a Friday, so I drove into London for it and went on to Herefordshire afterwards to spend the weekend with Megan and the children. The interview went well, but of course I had no idea how much competition there was for the post, so I was prepared for a letter of polite rejection. I was bowled over when I got back to my lodgings on the Sunday night to find a letter waiting for me from the Managing Director saying that he would like to see me again and wanted to meet Megan. He therefore invited both of us to meet his wife and himself for lunch at the Dorchester the following Friday. This was very exciting, a dramatic change of circumstances for both of us, making it possible for us to get married and go to India with the children and for me to take up a new and responsible senior post.

At that time the world of personal communications was still in the Stone Age. It was probably still a minority of homes which had a landline telephone, and mobile phones were more than forty years in the future. Megan and I had had to plan for the possibility that I might need to give her some urgent news, so she had given me the phone number of a neighbour which I could call on the Monday evening if necessary, and she would be there to take the call. I made the call from a call box and arranged for Megan to come up to London on the Thursday and stay in a guest house near Goodmayes. She was able to leave the children with her mother, who lived next door. By now I had had to spill the beans to my manager and get his agreement to my having most of Friday off to attend this vital meeting at the Dorchester. So I made a brief appearance at the office, collected Megan and drove into London. Megan had in her younger days, when she was a student nurse, had the good fortune to be entertained at high-class restaurants, so was not intimidated by an invitation to lunch at the Dorchester. For me it was very different, an awe-inspiring experience. I was totally unfamiliar with the world of luxury hotels and smart restaurants. I found that the most difficult part was managing the menu, which had a long list of mostly unfamiliar items. Fortunately, Billy Rooksby, the Managing Director, had some understanding of my problem and made helpful suggestions. He also chose the wines. Over lunch there was general discussion of the conditions in which we would be living in Bombay, but no particular discussion of the job. The letter I had received did not actually offer the job, so we had to assume that it should be construed as a conditional offer, dependent on our pleasing Billy Rooksby and his wife over lunch. Evidently all was well, because after lunch Mr Rooksby took me off in a taxi, leaving the two ladies at the Dorchester. We first went to the office in Curzon Street, where the retired Air Vice Marshal awaited us and Billy Rooksby and I signed two copies of a formal contract of employment between the Indian company and myself. We then went on to the offices of Cox & Kings, travel agents, in King Charles II Street, who normally dealt with travel arrangements for the Indian company. There Mr Rooksby booked for the whole family passages by ship from

Liverpool to Bombay in October 1960. We parted company and I telephoned my manager to tell him that the deal was done. I then took some minor pleasure in hailing a taxi and asking to be taken to the Rochester, where Megan was waiting for me. From there we went off to Herefordshire for the weekend.

From that point on there were several weeks of excitement and activity. I handed in my resignation from Ford, in whose employment I had spent only nine months. Notwithstanding this short stay, I was given a cheerful send off in a pub by my colleagues in Organisation Planning and a leaving present of an LP of a Brahms symphony. The first thing we had to do was to arrange to get married and for this we fixed a date of 10 September. I would have been content with a civil ceremony, but in deference to Megan's wishes we arranged with the Canon who was the priest at the church in the village of Eardisland where Megan lived, to be married there. To keep costs down we dispensed with the organist. It had to be a wedding on the cheap, as we did not have much money between us and no contributions from either of our respective families. My mother, who was by this time separated from my father, came with my two sisters, Margaret and Susan, and my brother Robin, ten years younger than me and in the RAF as an officer cadet, was my best man. Megan's mother, brother Derek, and two of her sisters, Gwyneth and Dilys, and their husbands lived locally. Another sister, Edna, and her husband came from Scotland and her brother Ken and his wife came from Lancashire. Canon Harmer was very generous in performing the ceremony cheerfully and pleasantly and foregoing his fee. We had a very modest party for the guests, champagne – or more likely a cheap sparkling wine – and a modest meal at the village pub, before we went off on a brief honeymoon to Borth on the Welsh coast, leaving Megan's children with her mother.

By mid-October 1960, everything was prepared for our departure to India. Megan had had the good fortune to be allocated a new small council house in the village of Eardisland in Herefordshire, which she had been living in for just over a year and into which I moved after we were married. We now vacated this and Megan moved the new furniture she had bought into store. We went with the children to visit Megan's sister and brother-in-law in Scotland and spent our last few days with my mother in Darwen, before travelling to Liverpool to board the *Caledonia*, the Anchor Line ship which was to take us to Bombay. For me it was just under a year since I had arrived back at Liverpool on an Elder Dempster ship from Freetown, Sierra Leone. Both of us had plenty of experience of international travel by sea in the years before the advent of the jet airliner sounded the death knell for sea travel as opposed to leisure cruising.

The total journey time to Bombay was twenty-two days. (I will stick to Bombay rather than the modern name Mumbai because that was the name of the city all the time we lived in India.) The ship was continuously at sea for the first nine days until we reached Port Said and began the transit of the Suez Canal. The Middle East was a new experience for both of us, the canal, the Sinai Desert, the Red Sea and Aden. Our first landfall in Asia was at Karachi, where the *Caledonia* spent a day unloading some passengers and cargo.

We arrived in Bombay early one hot morning. Harry Hardie, Office Director and previously Company Secretary, and his wife Sheila were there to meet us and there was a lorry to take our heavy baggage. Soon we were on our way by car to Mulund, location of the company's Head Office and one of its factories twenty miles out to the north east. After we cleared the docks and the centre of the city (known as the Fort Area) we were soon travelling on the Agra Road, just a two-lane highway, very congested, going through the industrial suburbs of North Bombay, passing factories, offices, apartments and large areas of slum dwellings. At Mulund, we drove past the company's factory, went underneath the four track railway from Bombay to Poona and central India and into Palmacres, the residential compound where Mr Rooksby and other senior executives of the company lived. Palmacres was an oasis of well-tended gardens and other greenery, with a swimming pool and tennis court, surrounded by a high concrete wall. The only exit was close to the railway line and Mulund Station. On the south side, the slum dwellings of the town of Mulund, came right up to the wall.

We were allocated the top floor of a two-storey apartment, the lower floor being occupied by Mr Swami, the Indian Works Director, his wife, Lily, and two teenage children, a girl, Gita, and a boy, Jagan. Sheila Hardie had taken a great deal of trouble to find servants for us – a cook, a bearer and a Christian nanny for the children – and she had also bought in supplies of food so that we could get started and did not need to go shopping. We had arrived on a Saturday, so we had the weekend to settle in before I started work on the Monday morning.

On Monday morning there was a Board meeting, chaired by Mr Rooksby, with Mr Swami, Harry Hardie, and the Sales Director. There were also two non-executive directors, one representing Associated Cement Ltd. An Indian company which had a 25% shareholding in the company, and the other the partner of Crawford Bailey, an old established firm of solicitors in Bombay who were legal advisers to the company. I attended the meeting as part of my initiation into the company's affairs and at a subsequent meeting soon afterwards was formally appointed Company Secretary.

The Congress government under Pandit Nehru which had governed India since independence in 1947 was strongly committed to socialist and even to some extent communist principles. In Soviet style the government committed the country to a series of five-year plans, setting out the path for industrial development in considerable detail. Railways, airlines, steel, mines and other areas of heavy industry were state owned. Industry generally continued to be privately owned by a mixture of Indian and foreign, including British, companies, but was very heavily regulated by central government. Production in many sectors had to be licensed by quotas and it was strictly illegal for a company to exceed its quota for the quantity of any item which it manufactured. India had a Companies Act very much based on the UK Companies Act, but with provisions added to it which were unique to India such as a requirement that the salaries of directors of major companies and any increases in their salaries must be approved by the Indian government's Company Law Department. Not only that, but any proposed increase had to be advertised in both English language and vernacular newspapers.

Another protectionist policy which did not always work to India's advantage was that of deliberately protecting domestic manufacture against imports. The government was ever keen to encourage domestic manufacture, and the effect of the policy would often be that if, for example, an Indian company began to manufacture typewriters in India, imports of typewriters might be prohibited altogether. High customs duties on imports were not considered to be an adequate means of protecting home-based industry. In some cases this meant that the Indian company faced no competition and could get away with making and selling products of inferior quality. The most egregious example of this kind of restriction was the ban on imports of cars. At this time just one make of car was manufactured in India by Hindustan Motors – the Ambassador, a medium-sized saloon based on the design of a long discontinued British Leyland model and still being made until recent years. Production of these was never enough to meet demand and the Indian government imposed a system of rationing. As an example of how this worked, Asbestos Cement Ltd had four factories in different parts of India and sales representatives covering the whole country from four regional offices attached to the factories. The company was allocated just one new car a year, far below its needs. As a result of the ban on imports there was a thriving market in second-hand cars, especially American models, which were expensive to maintain and were kept on the road long after they ought to have been scrapped.

Both the Union government and the governments of the States of India were keen to protect the rights of workers with an elaborate panoply of laws. Government officials and special labour courts had power to intervene in industrial disputes and settle in detail the pay and other conditions if the employees, unions and employers had difficulty in sorting things out by negotiation. One of the remarkable results of this protection was that the courts evolved a right of employees to a bonus from their employers, based on their profits and loss statements – a right which had no basis in any legislation. Another result was that it became difficult for employers to dismiss employees regardless of whatever misdemeanours they might have committed. Any dismissal had to be justified by evidence comparable to that required by a civil court and the employer had to hold an inquiry on the same lines as a court hearing and keep a detailed record.

On occasions I have heard apologists for India's notorious bureaucracy excuse it on the grounds that it is simply a legacy of the British Raj. This is nonsense for several reasons:

1. The five-year plans, the elaborate system of licensing of industrial production, the highly restrictive labour laws and the rest of the shackles placed on private industry were all introduced by legislation passed after independence. No doubt there was some bureaucracy in the days of the Raj but it was at a tolerable level and readily justifiable.
2. If there was any truth in the allegation the answer to it would be that India had by 1960, the year in which I arrived in India, been independent for thirteen years and there would have been ample time and opportunity to get rid of or amend any overly bureaucratic laws and practices. But the allegation was untrue.

3. The British Empire included many territories which were governed by elaborate systems of law and order based on British practice and which were all able to go their own ways and regulate their own affairs after independence. If one takes Singapore as an example, it was more or less completely created by the British as opposed to the case of India, where British rule was imposed on ancient civilisations. These origins did not prevent it from becoming one of the Asian tigers after independence and building up a thriving economy, a complete contrast to the sclerotic economy of India in the 1960s.

The basis for recruiting for Asbestos Cement Ltd a new Company Secretary with some legal background, but not necessarily a qualified lawyer, was mainly the need to have someone who could grapple with the complexities of India's labour laws as well as performing the normal duties associated with the office. I became aware that there were forty-six applicants for the post and have always assumed that the reasons for my being the successful candidate were that I had a law degree, though no professional qualification at this stage, and had also had five years' experience as an administrator with legal responsibilities in Sierra Leone. I had also had very brief experience of working in industry, but nine months at Ford probably did not count for a great deal. When I first got the job I told a Cambridge contemporary who was by now established as a professional accountant about it, and he was so shocked that he dropped the phone. He was clearly jealous and incredulous because he picked up the phone and said, "But, Harry, you don't know anything about being a company secretary!" I cheerfully admitted this but told him I was willing to learn. In smaller companies the jobs of finance director and company secretary are often combined, so this was the sort of position to which my friend might well in due course have aspired. I was certainly conscious that I would have a lot to learn and as a first step bought a textbook on company law which I read on the ship on the way to India.

The company had four factories in different parts of India, one at Mulund next to Head Office, one in Madhya Pradesh in Central India, one in Calcutta and another near Coimbatore in South India. All made the same range of asbestos cement building materials, mainly roofing sheets and drainpipes. The raw material was a mixture of cement, asbestos and water which was moulded into the required shape by various pieces of machinery or in some cases by hand. Because the mixture would soon set hard if left too long it was necessary and economical to keep production going in three shifts round the clock. As a result each factory had quite a large work force, so it was the responsibility of each Works Manager to ensure that continuous production was not disrupted by industrial disputes. That responsibility was necessarily delegated to local managers, but some help was needed from the centre to ensure that the company maintained proper labour relations practice at all four sites and to ensure that as far as possible practice was harmonised. I was therefore required, apart from fulfilling the normal duties of a Company Secretary, keeping the minutes of Board meetings etc., to be a central personnel manager. In retrospect, this was a daunting prospect for a newly arrived expatriate with no previous experience of India or of managing Indian labour or indeed of personnel management regarded as a particular skill.

I ought to say a little about asbestos, which at that time was used to make building materials, rope, brake linings and other products, because it was a great reinforcing agent. It was some years later, after I had left India, that its harmful effects in causing asbestosis became a cause for concern and led to its being banned for most uses. At Mulund, I lived with my family for over three years close to a factory using large quantities of asbestos every day and inevitably some of it as well as particles of cement got into the air, but I am happy to say that none of us ever experienced any harmful effects from this exposure.

For both Megan and myself comparisons between India and Sierra Leone were inevitable. Both are now members of the Commonwealth and Sierra Leone was still a colony, though it achieved independence just six months after our arrival in India. The British influence and tradition were strong in both countries and at that time both would have been classed as developing nations, though the experience of India was totally different from that of Sierra Leone. It seemed absurd to regard India as a developing country when to all outward appearances it was already well developed. It had cities such as Bombay and Calcutta with their assortment of factories making a huge range of goods. It had broad gauge and metre gauge railways providing long distance services across the nation and overcrowded commuter services by electrically hauled trains in the cities. Above all, it was the current incarnation of an ancient civilisation with its own languages, all with their own ancient scripts. It had an advanced education system and high rate of literacy. It had a large and sophisticated middle class, able to meet its own needs for doctors, engineers, lawyers, university teachers, accountants and managers and to export many highly qualified people to the United Kingdom and elsewhere.

It was reflections on these lines which led me to think about the reasons why I, an expatriate without any qualifications other than a law degree, had been selected to take up an appointment as Company Secretary of a fairly substantial and well established company in India. I think if I had been responsible for making the decision I would have preferred to recruit an Indian for the job, someone who already knew India as his own country, spoke one or more Indian languages and had previous experience of working in industry in India. There was no shortage of well qualified and very able Indians who would have been eligible. Another factor would have been cost saving. Expatriates had to be paid more to make it worth their while to leave their own countries, be provided with accommodation and be allowed periodic home leave with passages paid. I suppose that the main reason for recruiting an expatriate, apart from any particular factors which might have influenced the choice of me rather than any of the other candidates, was that the company was 75% British owned and already had a British managing director and other senior executives. However, in retrospect, I am sure that the recruitment of someone such as myself, new to India, its languages, culture and everything else about India, new also to anything more than a general notion of the duties of a Company Secretary either in India or anywhere else, must have caused some resentment among the company's Indian managers, though they were all too polite and deferential to let such feeling show.

The company was well established and faithfully served by sales and works managers and accountants each with many years' service. The company's functioning and prosperity depended on them. Living in India had its drawbacks – high taxation, prohibition, import restrictions – but with my family I enjoyed benefits to which expatriates tended to assume they were entitled: a luxurious furnished house or apartment, in our case in a park-like compound, servants and chauffeur-driven cars. Looking back now on the way of life we enjoyed fifty years ago I find it difficult to justify.

This was my second experience of life as an expatriate, following on from my five years as a bachelor Assistant District Commissioner in Sierra Leone, which I described in *Remote Corners*. There also I had lived a privileged existence, but there were important differences. Sierra Leone, in common with other neighbouring parts of West Africa, had had limited contact with the rest of the world, first on the coast from the end of the eighteenth century onwards, then in its interior in what is now referred to as the Scramble for Africa, the competition among Britain, France, Portugal, Germany and Spain to assert control over African territories in the last twenty years of the nineteenth century. Although the area adjacent to the Sahara Desert in what is now Mali was the seat of an ancient civilisation, this was not the case in the tropical rain forests nearer to the coast, where preliterate societies comprising mainly peasant farmers, fishermen or herdsmen were plagued by much internal strife and disorder. I was in Sierra Leone between 1954 and 1959. Some worthwhile progress had been made towards Africanisation of public services, but there was a long way to go. Administration of the Protectorate's twelve districts was dependent on expatriate District Commissioners and Assistant District Commissioners. There was just one black DC. The situation was similar in other departments, which were dependent on expatriate engineers, doctors and other professional people in varying degrees. So I never had the feeling then and do not have it now in retrospect, that there was a ready supply of intelligent and experienced Africans who could have replaced me. Our existence was privileged, but nowhere near so luxurious as the life which I later had with my family in India. We usually lived in government-provided houses in reservations on the edge of African towns. Basic furniture was supplied and the spacious compounds were created by clearing the bush around the houses, which were kept in reasonably trim condition by labourers paid out of public funds. But no cars other than those we bought for ourselves and no air-conditioned rooms. Basic salaries were the same for African and European officers, though the expatriates had the benefit of an additional allowance. We did of course, also have home leaves on a generous scale of one week back home for each month spent in Sierra Leone, and air or sea passages for home leave were paid for.

Hindi Classes

We gradually got used to the routines of daily living and working in India. Living at Mulund meant enjoying the semirural ambience of Palmacres but it had the disadvantage of having frequently to face the chaos and congestion of the Agra Road on a journey into the centre of Bombay which normally took over an hour. Only a limited range of groceries was available at Mulund, so Megan quite often had to go into Bombay to shop. I often had to go in on business and for some time travelled in early on two mornings a week to attend classes in Hindi. The main vernacular of Bombay, capital of the state of Maharashtra, is Marathi, but Hindi is widely spoken in the city, is the main language of Madhya Pradesh and other states, and is the lingua franca of northern India generally. The classes were organised by the Bombay Chamber of Commerce for the benefit of expatriate executives of member companies and held in the Chamber's offices opposite Ballard Pier. Our teacher was Mr Vaswani, a middle-aged Hindi munshi with many years' experience of teaching Hindi to foreigners. His teaching was geared to our needs in having to deal with mainly junior employees such as drivers and chowkidars (security staff) who might have little or no English. Managers, even fairly junior managers, would normally speak good English and work all the time in English. I have always had an aptitude for languages and I picked up basic Hindi fairly quickly. I found it useful to be able to have simple conversations with junior office staff, our servants and with ordinary people generally. As well as learning the spoken language we were introduced to the Devanagari script in which Hindi is written and which was to be seen everywhere – on advertising hoardings, buildings, buses and trains, sometimes with the same message in Roman script but often alone. There were also books and newspapers published in the Devanagari script. After some months of attending classes I was happy to take and pass the Lower Standard Hindi examination, a survival from the days of the British Raj, when newly arrived members of the Indian Civil Service had to learn and demonstrate proficiency in the language.

My fellow pupils were of different nationalities – British, Swiss, Irish and German – and all more or less the same age as me, with the exception of a British woman who was probably in her early forties and therefore in the view of Mr Vaswani entitled to slightly more deferential treatment. With all his years of teaching foreigners he spoke excellent idiomatic English, but went slightly astray in regularly addressing or referring to this woman as 'the Madame'. On one occasion when our teacher was briefly out of the room, she said to the rest of us, "If Mr Vaswani keeps referring to me as the Madame I am going to ask him, where are my girls?"

Working in India

I had two tours of duty in India with my family and a home leave in between. During my first tour I had to face a major industrial dispute which brought about the closure of the Mulund factory for some months when all the work force went on strike. Trouble was already brewing when I first arrived in Mulund. My recollection is that it arose from the employment of a large number of temporary workers and pressure from the union to have them all made permanent, which improved their pay and other benefits. For some time the union had been headed by a fairly mild man called Bapat, but the shop stewards felt that they needed someone rather more forceful and persuaded one R J Mehta, a well known Bombay Union firebrand, to take over. From this point on began a seemingly never ending series of meetings with Mehta, the Works Manager, Mr Sitaram, and senior officials in the office of the Bombay Commissioner of Labour. I have forgotten much of the detail of these meetings and it would in any case be tedious to relate. However, after some time Mehta decided to organise picketing demonstrations outside the main gate which was the entrance to both factory and head office. He made sure that there was no violence and that Head Office staff were not obstructed from entering and leaving, but only a narrow passageway was left open between the ranks of shouting workers. I and others from Palmacres walked to the office by crossing the railway lines and went home for lunch, so we had to face the mob four times a day. I never felt that there was any threat of personal violence but the experience was uncomfortable. Quite early on we sought an injunction in the Bombay City Civil Court to restrain the demonstrators and obtained an order which defined the physical limits which they had to observe. Mehta was most meticulous in making sure that the strikers did not step over the line and risk prosecution for contempt of court.

This was my first experience of going to court in India and I was agreeably impressed by the way the best traditions of the imperial legacy of English law were maintained. Judge and counsel wore gowns and bands but had sensibly long ago dispensed with wigs. The Bombay High Court was an old and dignified building in the Fort Area and the court rooms, though spacious and airy, were hot and sweaty. Pleas over the years from the local bar to have the building air conditioned had been unsuccessful. The hearing never went beyond the stage of obtaining an interim injunction on the basis of an affidavit which I swore, so there was no hearing of oral evidence which would have been necessary if the case had continued and a permanent injunction had been sought. The courtroom was crowded with a large number of the strikers and just a small number of people to represent the company, our barrister, by the name of Tijoriwala, the factory's works manager and personnel manager, and myself. We were heavily outnumbered but the proceedings were conducted in an orderly fashion. In the best tradition of the Chancery Division the judge called in a stenographer and began to dictate his judgement aloud as soon as the legal arguments on both sides ended.

Eventually, the dispute was settled, and again I do not recall the details of the settlement, and the factory resumed production to everyone's relief. One unfortunate aspect of the strike was that Mr Rooksby was retiring after long service with the company in India and the leaving function for him with the staff at Mulund was not attended by any members of the factory work force other than managers, as the strike was still on. After his many years of service with the company this obviously upset him. There was some concern during the strike that the work force might threaten the residents of Palmacres and/or bring Head Office to a standstill, which would have been seriously detrimental to the company's business. Plans were made to evacuate us all to accommodation in the centre of Bombay and to continue the work of Head Office from there, but happily the necessity to implement these plans was averted. I am happy to be able to record that in spite of all the sometimes acrimonious arguments with Metha and the shop stewards in the course of the dispute, my relations with all concerned remained friendly. Some months after the dust had settled I was invited to preside over a football match on the May Day (Labour Day) holiday on the recreation ground set aside for the employees at Mulund. It was a holiday and I walked across with Megan and the children to a very amiable reception. My only function was to start the match by kicking the ball and thereafter leaving everything to the players and the referee. I also made a brief speech in which I thanked the employees for their invitation. I had contemplated making it in Hindi, having by now made a passing acquaintance with the language, but my nerve failed me and I spoke in English, but asked Mr Talwalkrar, the factory personnel manager, to interpret for me.

Another important case which I had to deal with was one of trade mark infringement. The company's trade mark on the asbestos cement roofing sheets and drain pipes which were its products was EVEREST and it was well established in India as indicating products of the highest quality. One of our sales representatives in the north of India reported that a small back street company in Jaipur, Rajasthan, a very popular tourist destination, was making pipe joints bearing a superficial resemblance to those made by the company and bearing the name EVERBEST but with a very faint letter 'B'. Clearly, this was a case of trying to pass off these joints as made by Asbestos Cement Ltd. and a blatant infringement of the company's trade mark and the goodwill attached to it.

I visited Jaipur, and engaged a local attorney to act for us and threaten proceedings against the local people involved unless they desisted. They did not desist, so we issued a writ in the local civil court. Trade marks are a somewhat recondite branch of the law, but of vital importance to the businesses of many companies. In a relative backwater such as Jaipur, local lawyers and judges would be unfamiliar with the relevant law, so on the advice of our Bombay solicitors I engaged a prominent Parsee lawyer, Shavakshah, who had been previously the head of India's Trade Marks Registry and who now practised privately in this field. I went again to Jaipur with Shavakshah to prosecute our case, on the basis of my own affidavit and oral evidence about the company's Indian business and the quantity of business it did in and around Jaipur. The defendants were represented by counsel. I was given to understand that their business was owned by two partners, but neither of them came to court, leaving their affairs in the hands of a junior manager and counsel. The excuse was that they were not feeling well, but it is more likely that they were afraid of being shown up by such an eminent lawyer. We won the case and obtained an order requiring the defendants to cease using the offending mark and to destroy products bearing the mark and moulds for making any more products.

This was a worthwhile exercise and successful from the company's point of view. I enjoyed personally three visits in all to Jaipur and saw something of the palaces for which this former princely state is famous, including the Hawaii Mahal and the Amber Palace. The Rambagh Palace Hotel where we stayed in the city was a former home of the Maharajah of Jaipur. On one of my visits I drove with our local representative from Delhi to Jaipur and saw something of the desert of Rajasthan. Apart from the sightseeing, it was a pleasure and a privilege to come to know such a distinguished lawyer as Shavakshah. Megan and I became members of his social circle. He had a weekend villa in the Western Ghats, the range of mountains which runs down the west side of India, well out of Bombay and beyond Mulund. One Sunday we and another couple who were our guests were invited to the villa for lunch and tea, where we joined a lively family party. Many Bombay Parsees were fanatical bridge players, and some members of our host's family were playing bridge while we were there, though we were not under any pressure to join in. It was just an enjoyable social occasion.

Setting up a School

Palmacres Mulund was a small cocooned residential colony for the directors, Company Secretary and one or two other senior staff with their families twenty miles outside the city of Bombay. All were expatriates with the exception of the Works Director, Mr Swami, and the company doctor, Dr. Sanjana. Mr Swami had two teenage children, a boy and a girl, who both attended schools in Bombay. The rest of us had between us six children between 3 and 5 years old. Mulund was in the middle of a group of industrialised suburbs, several of which had residential colonies similar to Palmacres. One of these was a colony housing the works manager and other executives of a subsidiary company of GKN, a manufacturer of nuts, bolts, screws and other metal products, whose parent company is based in Birmingham. The GKN manager had established a small pre-school/primary school for the children of resident

Harry Mitchell and mother in Cambridge – Graduation, June 1953.

Harry Mitchell, Assistant District Commissioner, on trek in Sierra Leone 1957

Cover of Harry Mitchell's first book, describing experiences in Sierra Leone 1954-59

Megan and Harry Mitchell on our Wedding Day, 10th September 1960, in Eardisland, Herefordshire

Harry Mitchell and Megan, Bombay 1962

Harry Mitchell and Megan, 25th wedding anniversary,
Tiltyard restaurant, Hampton Court Palace

Harry Mitchell playing the piano

Harry Mitchell on appointment as Company Secretary of
Wellcome November 1976

Harry Mitchell being presented to King Juan Carlos of Spain.
Board meeting of Wellcome in Madrid in 1985

Harry Mitchell on appointment as Queen's Counsel, ceremony
at the House of Lords April 1987

Harry Mitchell and daughter Kamini. Hampton Court Palace 1990

Harry Mitchell and Megan, in the grounds of Hampton Court Palace 1990

Harry Mitchell as Chairman of Sarsen Housing association, Devizes, laying the foundation stone of Sarsen's head office building February 1997

Harry Mitchell as Chairman of Sarsen Housing Association and with a tenant and the Princess Royal at the ceremonial opening of Sarsen's housing estate at a former mental hospital in Devizes

*Harry Mitchell and Megan in the lobby of Raffles
Hotel Singapore during a cruise*

*Mitchell siblings and spouses. Back row HM, Megan, brother in law Rex
(now deceased) brother Robin, sister in law Geneviève,
brother in law Stewart. Front row sisters Margaret and Susan.*

managers and was also happy to accommodate children of managers of other companies in the area. The school catered for perhaps ten children who were taught by an Anglo-Indian teacher. For a while the Palmacres children went there and were taken daily by a company car. We decided that it would be a good idea to start our own school when the population of eligible children increased from four to six. It fell to me to set up the school, recruiting a teacher and fitting out a building and arranging to charge monthly fees to be paid by the parents. We had in the grounds of Palmacre a building intended originally as a small club house. This building had one room for a billiard table which was used only occasionally at weekends, but the other rooms were empty and were readily converted for use by a one class school. I advertised for a teacher and had a good response. I recruited a young Indian Christian woman who had already trained as a teacher.

The school did not get off to a good start. The mother of two of the children, wife of one of the resident directors, began complaining about the teaching and everything about the school within the first two days and would rant on the telephone at me for half an hour or more at a time. I cannot now remember all the detail, but I did not attempt to remember the detail at the time as the list of complaints was never ending. To make matters worse she and her husband went to see the teacher without telling me and bullied her. The teacher, Miss Vaz, held her ground very well, but was greatly upset by the way these people treated her. I was in the unfortunate position of being the Company Secretary, not on the board and having to fend off complaints from a director. I appealed to the Managing Director to intervene to put these people in their place. He was willing to act at first but then his courage failed him and he left me to cope on my own. This unpleasant state of affairs was resolved after a while when the director and his wife decided that the Palmacres School was not good enough for their children, whom they therefore withdrew and transferred to another school at Juhu, some miles away. This meant providing a company driver to take them there and bring them back five days a week, but so far as I was concerned it was a great relief.

After the school had been functioning for a few months I was approached by an Indian manager working for one of the pharmaceutical companies based close to Mulund, who wished to have his four-year-old son admitted as a pupil. So far as I was concerned the boy would be a welcome addition to our numbers but I decided that to be on the safe side I ought to get the approval of the Managing Director. The Rooksbys never had any children and Mr Rooksby felt the need to enquire about how a boy from an Indian family would fit in. The parents spoke English but at home they spoke Hindi and their son was not yet familiar with English. Mr Rooksby regarded this as a total bar on accepting the boy but I explained that young children picked up languages very quickly and I did not think that the boy's initial lack of English would be a problem. Mr Rooksby agreed with some reluctance that I could accept the boy on condition that I first satisfied myself that he was suitable. This meant that I had to take on the unrealistic task of interviewing a four-year-old before admitting him as a pupil, but I carried out my instructions and accepted the boy.

Once the initial problem described above was overcome, the school was a happy place and the children were well taught the rudiments of the three Rs. In the course of 1962, Miss Vaz married and became pregnant. By now I had resigned and would be leaving India on 1 January 1963. Mrs Correa, as our teacher was now known, persuaded me that she would be able to resume teaching not long after her baby was born and as a stop gap arrangement I should take on a young friend of hers to look after the class in her absence. I met the young woman and agreed to this arrangement. In the event Mrs Correa had her baby just before Christmas and her locum took over the class in early January. I am sorry to have to admit that the locum was not a success and John Stedman, a sales manager living in

Palmacres, who took over responsibility for the school, had to sort things out. Not one of my better decisions. However, everything went well up to Christmas. Mr Rooksby insisted on dressing up as Father Christmas and visiting the school driving a tractor from the factory to distribute presents to the children, but was recognised by some of the children. Mrs Correa, heavily pregnant, organised the children to put on a nativity play for the parents, which made a happy ending for Megan and myself for our three years in Palmacres.

Travels Around India

My work involved a fair amount of travelling around India, visiting the company's scattered factories. For the most part this meant travelling by the services operated by Indian Airlines, a nationalised company which had a state monopoly of internal air services. External services were operated by Air India. Indian Airlines had possibly the world's largest fleet of ageing DC3 (Dakota) aircraft for shorter haul services and also had Vickers Viscount turboprop aircraft for longer hauls such as Bombay to Calcutta, a journey of 900 miles which took about four hours. The DC3s were beginning to be replaced by the Dutch-built Fokker Friendships, which operated the service I used for my journeys between Bombay and Jaipur. I have vivid memories of the last journey I ever made in a DC3 from Allahabad, a major city in the state of Uttar Pradesh to Delhi. It was a hopping service with intermediate stops at Kanpur and Lucknow. This was just before the start of the monsoon and departure from Allahabad was delayed because of an electrical storm. The DC3 was a wartime American built twin-piston engine transport aircraft, and was not pressurised. In consequence, it could not fly higher than 5000 feet, which meant that it could not avoid the pre-monsoon turbulence. The plane called at Kanpur and then took off for Lucknow. It was a very bumpy journey for a while, but suddenly the plane hit what I assume was an air pocket and dropped like a stone. In the passenger cabin there was chaos. Bags, brief cases and other items on the open luggage racks were thrown out. The plane carried about fifty passengers and one stewardess; the catering arrangements consisted of a large tin trunk at the rear of the plane, which was overturned and emptied its contents, cups, saucers, milk, sugar and everything else, in an undisciplined torrent down the aisle. The plane was being bumped up and down and from side to side and I could hear the engines groaning as the pilot struggled to keep it on a level setting. I could feel the palms of my hands sweating with fear and I swore to myself that if I got out alive I would never fly in a DC3 again – and I never did. The plane called at Lucknow but there was further dangerous turbulence at the start of the last stage of its journey from Lucknow to Delhi. As a result, the pilot landed at an Indian Air Force base at Agra, where we all waited on the ground until the weather improved enough for us to complete our fraught journey. We reached Delhi very late, but thankful to be still alive and in one piece.

The 1960s were the start of the jet era and Air India took delivery of its first jets, Boeing 707s, while we were in India. At first, the pilots were being trained and doing circuits and bumps, landing and taking off from Santa Cruz Airport, then Bombay's only airport. Soon, they were starting to operate international services from Delhi, but Indian Airlines had a regular charter flight by Air India Boeing 707 which went from Bombay to Delhi every evening. The excitement of seeing this plane, much bigger than any previous civil airliner seen in India, with its noisy jet engines, taking off and landing at Santa Cruz, attracted huge crowds of sightseers to a vantage point in front of the terminal building. I had the privilege of travelling first class, which did not mean anything when travelling in the smaller planes, which did not have any first-class seats, so I greatly enjoyed the comfort of the first-class cabin in the 707 when I made my first journey in a passenger jet on a trip to Delhi.

Journeys by train in India were always a memorable experience. Mulund was on the busy four-tracked electrified main line out of Bombay for trains to most of central and eastern India, including Calcutta and Poona. The line also carried crowded and frequent commuter services which I occasionally used at off peak times as a relief from the tedium of long car journeys along the Agra Road. The commuter trains were electric multiple units with automatic sliding doors, but the doors were invariably permanently jammed open with passengers hanging out precariously at busy times. Bombay's suburban train services were the subject of a recent series of television documentaries, from which it was soon apparent that overcrowding was worse than ever, doors still jammed permanently open, passengers standing on couplings between coaches, and sitting on the roof. People are killed on Bombay's railways every day, some of them passengers who have lost their precarious hold on part of the train; others pedestrians who use the tracks as footpaths or cross busy lines and fail to avoid being hit by trains.

I sometimes had to take longer journeys, particularly to the company's factory at Kymore in Madhya Pradesh in Jabalpur District. There was no air service to Jabalpur or anywhere else conveniently near, so I took the evocatively named Howrah Mail, a trunk express from Bombay to Calcutta with numerous stops on the way. The station for Kymore was Jukehi, twenty hours and about 700 miles from Bombay. The Howrah Mail always had an air-conditioned coach in which travel was more expensive than first class. In first class a traveller would be cooled by an electric fan, but air conditioning made for a much more comfortable journey in the heat. Each compartment could accommodate two people and the seats were convertible into two bunk beds for night travel. Trains in India did not then and perhaps still do not have corridors linking coaches with each other, so as to eliminate the considerable likelihood that the first, second and air conditioned coaches would be invaded by passengers from third class. This meant that it was not possible to walk along to the dining car for a meal. Fortunately, on a long journey there were numerous stops and the system was that a passenger would ask the steward to bring him a meal at a station further along the line such as Jabalpur or Jhansi, which he would name. The food was fairly basic, cooked on a wood burning stove and was no longer so hot as it ought to be by the time it reached you. On one visit to Kymore I was taken ill with hepatitis, so the long journey back to Bombay was something of a trial. I ordered breakfast, and when it came the white of the fried egg on the plate was delicately ringed with soot, which made me feel even worse and I was unable to eat anything.

Hill Stations

On two occasions I went with my family and our nanny to Matheran for brief holidays which we all loved. This was a hill station in the western Ghats built in the days of the British Raj and much favoured by successive governors of the then Bombay State. We stayed in a basic but comfortable hotel. It had no flush lavatories, so women sweepers had to be in attendance to take the buckets away when the need arose. On one of our visits I had the pleasure of a chance meeting with Mr Vaswani, my Hindi teacher, and was able to introduce him to my family. Matheran was accessible only by a narrow gauge railway from Neral on the main line or by horse or on foot. There was no motor road to it. The railway climbed up the steep sides of the mountain through many twists and turns, the trains rarely travelled at more than walking pace and passengers were often pestered by large numbers of children who ran alongside begging for money. The town was on a mountain top at about 800 metres and commanded spectacular panoramic views in several directions. It was set in forest and the main attractions were the cool weather, a relief from the heat of the plains, the scenery, and walks along the numerous wide footpaths cut through the forest. It had been favoured at one time for tiger shooting and we saw in our small hotel at least one old photograph of a British sahib accompanied by his Indian shikars, sporting a rifle and standing proudly behind a dead tiger at his feet – not the kind of sporting activity which would be approved nowadays. From photographs I have seen on the Internet it is obvious that Matheran has been modernised in some ways and is now accessible by road and cable car, but the railway still runs. Wikipedia tells me that although there is now a road, the resort itself is still free of motor traffic. It is ninety kilometres from Bombay and 120 from Poona and because of its proximity to these two cities is a much favoured mountain resort.

Another hill station which I enjoyed visiting and which Megan visited with me at the end of our stay in India was Ootacamund (Ooty for short) in the Nilgiris (Blue Mountains) in South India. It is still served by a steam operated narrow gauge mountain railway, but on both visits I travelled by road. Ooty is at an elevation of over 7000 feet and is set among rolling hills and tea gardens. It has a famous club house, very much a legacy of the British Raj, owing its fame to the claim that the game of snooker was invented there. It had and possibly still has a hunt whose prey is jackals rather than foxes. On the wall there was a table updated every year giving the name of the Master of the Ooty Hounds every year from early in the 19th century, but for the years 1857-1859 there is no name, simply the entry 'The Mutiny', clearly a period when the club's routine ceremonies and enjoyable diversions were disrupted.

Prohibition

Prohibition imposed a damper on expatriate social life in India. On the insistence of Mahatma Gandhi the Constitution of India incorporated a commitment by all the states of the Union to adopt policies of banning the sale and consumption of alcohol, in many ways a superfluous requirement because in general most Indians, Hindu or Muslim, do not drink. However, the commitment was taken seriously by some of the states, including the former Bombay State under its then Chief Minister, Morarji Desai, who later became Finance Minister of India. (Morarji Desai was an ultra-puritan devotee of Mahatma Gandhi and was notoriously alleged to make a regular practice of drinking his own urine.) The state of Bengal by contrast, with its communist government, was unwilling to comply but told the Indian government that it would do so if the latter would meet the cost of enforcement of prohibition and make good the loss of revenue earned from taxes on the sale of alcohol. Clearly this was an impossible demand to meet and Bengal never did introduce prohibition. Before our arrival in Bombay the former Bombay State had been divided into the two linguistic states of Maharashtra and Gujarat, both of which continued to enforce prohibition.

As foreign residents, Megan and I were entitled to permits which allowed us a monthly ration of alcoholic drinks, in Megan's case three units and in mine four. One unit entitled the permit holder to buy one bottle of spirits, three bottles of wine or nine bottles of beer. Beer was expensive, but cheaper than wine or spirits, so we invariably spent our units on beer, which surprisingly enough in view of prohibition, was actually manufactured in India at a brewery in the Himalayas. So far as I recall, there was only one liquor store in Bombay, and visiting it to buy the monthly ration was a daunting experience. Each of us had to present our permits to the clerk behind the counter. It was a strict requirement that the permit holder had to present his or her own permit when making the purchase, so each of us had to make a separate journey for the purpose. Megan usually combined a visit to the liquor store with a shopping trip. The clerk would enter in his ledger and also on the permit itself details of the purchase and those details were also checked and recorded by a uniformed civil servant, an excise inspector, who was permanently based in the store. There were no pubs and the clubs were not allowed to supply alcoholic drinks. One or two of the major hotels had permit rooms, open only to permit holders. You could take your permit with you and order drinks, details of which had to be entered on the permit by the barman. As in the case of the liquor store there was a uniformed excise inspector keeping his own official record of transactions. It was a decidedly sobering experience.

The laws on prohibition in the state of Maharashtra made provision for granting permits to Indian nationals who were able to obtain medical certificates to the effect that they were alcoholics, but I do not recall ever meeting anyone who claimed to qualify or who had actually been granted such a permit. Of course, Indian trains and internal airlines were obliged to avoid serving alcohol, but there was an interesting exception in the case of the Indian Airlines Service from Bombay to Colombo, Sri Lanka, calling at Madras (now Chennai) en route. Indian Airlines was at pains to advertise that there was a bar service between Madras and Colombo, that being an international sector tacked on to a domestic flight.

Poverty in India

For the first few days after arrival Megan and I stayed at Mulund, but on our second weekend there decided to go out to a cinema, which meant a long journey into Bombay in one of the company's cars with a company driver. Bombay has always been the main centre of the Indian film industry, normally referred to nowadays as Bollywood and the city had several modern cinemas showing foreign and Indian films. I have no recollection of what we saw, but vividly remember the journey home at about 10pm. We were astonished and appalled to see the hundreds of bodies, mostly wrapped in white garments, sleeping on the pavements, having no other home in the city.

Mass poverty and homelessness are a feature of all Indian cities. People make their homes on pavements, on the platforms of railway stations or inside concrete pipes left by the side of the road sometimes for years before they are eventually used as part of a new water supply or sewage extension. In the crowded streets of the city there were many beggars, sometimes children who had had their hands deliberately amputated to arouse the pity of passersby, who had to hand over to their masters whatever *baksheesh* they had been able to collect. Those who are a little more fortunate than the pavement-dwellers erect for themselves makeshift *bustees* – homes of corrugated iron sheets, cardboard, plastic and whatever other materials they can find. They occupy any land which may be vacant and often create permanent settlements there. In a film on television recently about Indian railways there were sequences showing the problems faced by the railway management which was trying to increase the capacity of Bombay's desperately overloaded suburban lines by adding an extra pair of tracks on land already owned by the railways but long since occupied by thousands of *bustee*-dwellers. The railway police were given the unenviable job of clearing the land to enable the work to be started and were instructed to do the job as peacefully as possible so as to avoid riots. It is notorious that some of the slums become in effect permanent settlements. Makeshift shacks are built which trespass on land over which those making them have neither legal title nor planning permission. Within the city of Bombay the slum of Dharavi, which reaches right up to the perimeter fence of the city's main airport, is estimated to house around 600,000 people.

India was already a crowded country when we lived there. During our time in India a census was held which produced a total population figure of 428 million. The population now, just over fifty years later, is almost triple that – the figures are frightening.

Astrology

Belief in astrology has always been a powerful influence in India. In particular, astrologers are invariably consulted when marriages are being arranged and the horoscopes of bride and groom have to be compared. Sometimes we received invitations to attend Indian weddings in Bombay and it was not unusual to note that odd times such as 9.21 or 10.33am were given as the time for the actual ceremony, that having been fixed by the astrologers who had been consulted. While we lived at Mulund there was much concern about an *ashtagrahi*, a very rare astrological event of eight planets in conjunction. There were considerable concerns that this might presage some terrible catastrophe. Wealthy locals paid considerable sums to priests to hold propitiation ceremonies involving drumming all night long which we could hear from our bungalow. Although we did not have any real concerns it was a mild psychological relief the following morning when the sun rose and nothing terrible had happened overnight.

In April 1961, the USSR achieved the first manned space flight by Yuri Gagarin in a Vostok 1 spacecraft. This of course was sensational news worldwide and I experienced a significant Indian slant on the event. I was travelling into Bombay by car with one of the company's Assistant Works Managers, a young graduate engineer. We discussed the event and he expressed concern that if man began to put so many vehicles into space, these could affect the motions of the planets *and thus affect human destiny*. I found it astonishing that such a well-educated man with mathematical and scientific training could be so influenced by a wholly unscientific system of belief. Out of politeness I limited my response to pointing out that no spacecraft could be big enough or weighty enough to have any influence at all on the orbits of the planets or their satellites.

Goa and Kashmir

When we arrived in India in 1960, Goa was still a Portuguese colony and Portugal had refused Indian demands to surrender the territory to India. The territory had been annexed by Portugal in 1510 and had never been part of British India, to which India and Pakistan and later Bangladesh, were successor states. India therefore had no lawful claim to Goa, but that did not stop the Nehru government from demanding its surrender. Attempts were made in the Indian press to make out that there was a subversive resistance movement in Goa against continued Portuguese rule, but they were never convincing. Nehru I recall said on one occasion that his patience with the Portuguese was exhausted, an ominous echo of a speech made by Hitler before his troops marched into Czechoslovakia in 1939.

In December 1961, the Indian Army invaded Goa and there was no resistance. The Portuguese governor knew that the odds were overwhelmingly in India's favour and did not want to give any orders that would result in violent resistance and loss of life. Goa in due course became a state of India and Portugal long ago abandoned its claims. I do not know what is taught in Indian schools about the way in which Goa became part of the Union of India, but I felt sure at the time that it was not the wish of the people of Goa that this should happen and had this impression confirmed by conversations in later years with Goan Indians who had memories of the invasion.

India's history since independence in 1947 has been dominated by its dispute with Pakistan about Kashmir, which has been the cause of three wars between the two neighbours. At the time of independence it was up to the rulers of the many princely states which coexisted with British India to opt to join one of the two new countries. In the case of Kashmir, the Maharajah was a Hindu though a majority of the population was Muslim. His choice of India led to the first of the three wars and the dispute remains unresolved to this day. There is no agreed boundary between the two sectors of the divided state, merely a line of military demarcation. India's first Prime Minister, Pandit Nehru, refused to accept the call by the United Nations for a referendum by the people of Kashmir to allow them to choose whether their state should be part of India or of Pakistan, obviously because he must have been well aware that the result of voting by a majority Muslim population would have been a choice to accede to Pakistan. To date there has been no referendum.

Another incident of India's post-independence history which is not to its credit as a supposedly peace-loving nation concerns Hyderabad, the largest and most powerful of the princely states. The Nizam of Hyderabad in 1947 declared his intention of remaining independent and refused to accede to the Union of India. In 1948, there was some agitation against the Nizam fomented by the Congress and communist parties. The Indian Army invaded Hyderabad in what was known as Operation Polo and referred to by the politicians in language which would have been worthy of Orwell's *1984* as a 'Police Action'. As in the case of Goa the state had never been part of British India, though there was the difference that it had entered into a treaty with the East India Company in 1798, under which the state accepted the protection of the British Indian Army, units of which were stationed within its borders. The Nizam had to capitulate and sign the Instrument of Accession, under which he was appointed Princely Governor of the State.

Kashmir was quiescent during the time we were in India, but the security of India was jeopardised in 1962 by Chinese invasions on the country's northwest and northeast frontiers in areas where the boundary between the two countries had never been clearly demarcated. This was a particularly anxious time for us. We had been on leave in the United Kingdom and news of the invasion broke when we were on a ship returning to Bombay. There was a great deal of patriotic fervour and concern in India and there were anti-Chinese demonstrations. I can recall a bizarre photograph in one of the local newspapers of Indian women in saris who had volunteered to join the defence forces, bearing rifles on their shoulders. Fortunately, the Chinese obviously had very limited territorial ambitions and there was no major threat to India's cities. However, the invasion coincided with the threat of nuclear war brought about by the Cuban missile crisis, so the prospect of Armageddon began to look threateningly close.

Departure

There was much to like and enjoy about India, but it had its drawbacks. It has always proudly and with justification boasted of being the world's most populous democracy, but it also had the world's most sclerotic bureaucracy and life there was restricted by the limitations imposed on the freedom of companies in the private sector to run their businesses in the way they wished and by prohibition and other impediments on personal life of which I have written.

In 1962, I was able to return to the United Kingdom on leave. Megan left early with the children and I travelled home via Beirut for a rendezvous at Vienna's airport. I made a short stop in Beirut, where I arrived from Delhi late at night. The following morning I awoke in my hotel room to a great feeling of freedom. I was of course now on holiday, in itself an emancipating experience, but I also had a feeling of relief from the daily restrictions of life in India, comparable in some ways to the sensations which privileged people living under communist regimes in Eastern Europe must have felt on odd occasions when they were able to travel to the West; though not so dramatic as the ecstatic feelings which were evoked by the collapse of the Berlin Wall.

The quasi-communist apparatus of state control included notoriously high progressive rates of personal taxation. Income tax was already levied at punitively high rates by 1962, but the Chinese invasion in that year led to an urgent need for increased spending on defence and resulted in an extra surcharge being imposed. Wealthy citizens were subject to wealth tax and expenditure tax as well as income tax, but my own earnings and those of directors and other senior colleagues in the company never made any of us liable to be assessed for either of these, so I am happily ignorant of how they worked. It was sometimes reported in the financial pages that the combined effect of these taxes on individuals liable to be assessed for them meant that they could be taxed in any particular tax year for a sum greater than their actual income for the year, which meant that they would have to sell investments to meet their tax liabilities and sell more investments to cover their living costs. I am sure that many wealthy Indians succeeded in reducing their liabilities by lawful or unlawful means, but for people like myself, well paid but subject to an Indian equivalent of PAYE, the rates of tax were onerous.

Apart from levels of tax, the consideration which decided Megan and myself to leave India was the need in the near future to make provision for educating the children in the United Kingdom. By the time we left in January 1964, Kamini was almost seven and Howard was five. We had been able to make reasonable provision for their primary education and enjoyed the luxury of a company school in the compound at Palmacres, described earlier. Our single Indian teacher provided an excellent primary education for the children, but going on to secondary education would have been more difficult and would inevitably have meant putting the children into boarding schools in the UK.

It was with much regret that I resigned my position as Company Secretary of Asbestos Cement Ltd and embarked with my family on the *Orcades*, a P&O liner bound for Tilbury, on 1 January 1964. In the course of the voyage I spent a good deal of time with my portable typewriter, typing out job applications in response to advertisements which we had picked out from various newspapers. Megan and I were assigned to a table in the dining room which was presided over by the ship's chief electrical engineer, a cheerful and good-humoured Scot. The children had meals with other children and were now old enough to go to meals on their own, whereas on the voyage out in 1960, one of us had had to go with them. Our table companions were three elderly widows who had joined the ship in Sydney and were returning to the UK to visit their relations. I regret to say that we did not find them the most stimulating company and we sometimes envied our table host who seemed as the voyage progressed to have to deal with an increasingly frequent incidence of ship's electrical maintenance emergencies which prevented him from joining us at mealtimes.

On our leave from India in 1962, we had bought a small house in Hereford, in Megan's home county, and were able to go straight there when we arrived back home on 17 January 1964. I then faced the daunting task of finding a suitable job in the UK, which took me some eight months. But that is another story.

NATIONALISATION OF THE AIRCRAFT INDUSTRY

One of Tony Blair's achievements in establishing New Labour with important differences from Old Labour was the removal of Clause Four from the Labour Party's constitution. This was the clause which committed the party in government to ensuring public ownership of the 'commanding heights' of the national economy and which had led Labour governments from 1945 onwards to nationalise as public monopolies the railways, coal mines, steel and electricity generation. The Labour government under Harold Wilson which took office in 1974 had committed itself in its manifesto to nationalise the aircraft and shipbuilding industries and a Bill to achieve this objective was put before Parliament in 1975. Rolls Royce, the aero engine manufacturers, had already been nationalised by Ted Heath's Conservative government in 1971, following that company's financial collapse in February of that year. (See the chapter on '*My Life in the Law*' on this subject.) So far as the aircraft industry was concerned, the two main companies identified for nationalisation were Hawker Siddeley Aviation Limited (HSA) and British Aircraft Corporation Limited (BAC). These were the two major aircraft manufacturers in Britain, formed in the early 1960s under pressure from the government from a large number of smaller companies. The objective of the Bill was to take over and merge these two companies and two other companies, Hawker Siddeley Dynamics and Scottish Aviation, into a single state-owned corporation, British Aerospace. British Aerospace was formed as a nationalised corporation under the Aircraft and Shipbuilding Industries Act in 1977 and was privatised under the Thatcher government starting in 1981. It continues to exist under the name BAE Systems.

Nationalisation was opposed by the companies affected, though they had to accept that it was going to happen and do what they could to protect their shareholders' and employees' interests. As legal manager of HSA, it fell to me to study the Bill, draw the attention of management to its detailed provisions and follow its progress through the various stages in the legislative process. The company made common cause with BAC in opposing the Bill and recruiting opposition MPs in support. The main sponsor of the Bill was Tony Benn, Secretary of State for Industry, and the main responsibility for seeing the Bill through the House of Commons fell to Gerald Kaufmann, his Minister of State. The opposition was led by Michael Heseltine, supported by Norman Tebbit, Tom King, and others, with whom I had a certain amount of contact.

I have always been a floating voter, but for the purposes of looking after the company's interests and my own I had to side with the Conservative opposition to the Bill. Before the Bill appeared I was lent by HSA's General Manager a copy of a paper which Tony Benn had presented to Harold Wilson as a proposal for the manner in which nationalisation should be effected. Benn was MP for Bristol South East and the paper had been written by some of his academic friends at Bristol University. True to this provenance it was written in the form of a PhD thesis, complete with detailed references. It began by assuming that there was no longer any need to make a case for nationalisation, which must now be taken as accepted as a necessary objective and that all that had to be considered was how to go about it. The proposal amounted to setting out a paradigm for a new version of industrial democracy for a socialist state for the last quarter of the twentieth century. Sadly, I was unable to keep a copy and can record only what I remember of the paper. It was clear that the authors knew nothing about the aircraft industry and did not regard it as important to find out anything about it. Their main proposal was that the new corporation should be governed by a committee of worker representatives, each elected by one of the twenty or so wards into which the factories and offices of the corporation would be divided for this purpose. The intention clearly was that the elected representatives would be for the most part from the shop floor and *would have the power to hire and fire the management* – a topsy-turvy world indeed. This might have been a suitable model for some form of local government, but was ridiculously impractical for a large corporation which would have to earn its keep by designing, manufacturing and selling civil and military aircraft. In retrospect it is alarming to reflect that this absurd scheme was seriously put forward by the Secretary of State responsible for industry, a prominent politician who had at one stage been a candidate for leadership of the Labour Party and who could conceivably without too much stretch of the imagination have become Britain's Prime Minister. Happily, it did not find favour with Harold Wilson and the Nationalisation Bill was drafted in similar fashion to the statutes which had previously been enacted for bringing major industries into public ownership.

Uproar in the House of Commons

The Bill completed its committee stage in the House of Commons and a debate on Report Stage was set for 26 May 1976. I obtained a ticket for the Strangers' Gallery for the event, took my seat there in the evening and was surprised to find that the House was in a state of uproar. An important point of order on the Bill had been raised the previous day by Robin Maxwell-Hyslop, MP for Tiverton, and the Speaker, George Thomas (later ennobled as Lord Tonypandy), had retired with the Leader of the House, Michael Foot, to consider the point and take advice before he could make a ruling on it.

The point of order was that the Bill, which had come before the House as a public Bill, was properly a hybrid Bill and should therefore be referred to a Select Committee or Joint Committee of the House of Commons in accordance with the normal procedure for dealing with hybrid Bills. I need to explain, without going into too much boring detail, the basis on which the point of order was raised. The Bill covered both the aircraft and shipbuilding industries and the point related to the definition of a shipbuilding company for the purposes of the Bill. The name of such a company was to be included in the schedule for nationalisation if on 31 July 1974 it had an interest in a shipyard which had completed ships to a total of a minimum of 15,000 gross tons during the three years up to that date. Mr Maxwell-Hyslop drew attention to the fact that one company, Yarrow Shipbuilders, had been included in the schedule but a competitor company, Marathon Shipbuilding, which he claimed fell properly within the definition, had not. It appeared that the reason for excluding Marathon from inclusion was that at the material date of 31 July 1974, it was completing a vessel intended for use as an oil rig, which was, in the view of the draftsman of the Bill, not a ship as defined. Mr Maxwell-Hyslop contended that the vessel did fall within the definition of a ship in accordance with the Bill and therefore Marathon Shipbuilding had been improperly excluded from the Bill. For the Bill to be a public Bill it could not treat some people or companies falling within the same definition in a different fashion from others, so in this case if Marathon was to continue to be excluded the Bill must be treated as a hybrid Bill, which would give Yarrow Shipbuilders an opportunity to complain to the Select Committee that they had been treated unfairly in being nationalised while their competitor Marathon Shipbuilding was left in private ownership.

This was obviously a momentous point of order. If it was ruled that the Bill was hybrid that could mean that there would be delays in the progress of the Bill, as a Select Committee would have to be appointed to consider objections from aircraft or shipbuilding companies facing the prospect of nationalisation and from any other interested parties. The government might in that situation decide that it must abandon the Bill and leave the companies concerned in private ownership. This was obviously an appealing prospect for the companies concerned, their shareholders and at least some of their employees – including myself. When I took my seat in the Strangers' Gallery the consultation on the point of order was still under way outside the chamber. The House had not adjourned and the members were killing time by talking about anything they liked, just to keep the proceedings going. Eventually, the Speaker and Michael Foot returned to the Chamber and there was a palpable rise in tension and excitement. I could feel the palms of my hands sweating as the Speaker began his ruling in his strong Welsh accent. George Thomas, after brief, preliminaries said: "After long and anxious thought I now rule that the Bill under discussion is *prima facie* hybrid." There were immediate Opposition cheers and from this point on the House was in a state of continuous uproar. Michael Foot's response to the ruling as recorded in *Hansard* is worth quoting in full:

*"In view of your [**i.e. the Speaker's**] statement, it is clearly impossible for the House of Commons to proceed with this Bill today. But may I make it also equally clear – and I hope the House will agree with this – that the House should have the earliest possible opportunity of deciding how we proceed with the Bill.*

The jobs and the livelihood of many people are involved – [Interruption] We at least, Mr Speaker, are not prepared to put those jobs and the livelihood of people at risk. Therefore, Mr Speaker, the government propose to table, as first business tomorrow, a motion which the House can decide to accept or reject, whichever it wishes. It is for the House to decide. But the Motion will have the full backing of the government. Our motion reads as follows: "That, in view of the grave consequences for the industries concerned and for those employed in them of further delay and uncertainty in further proceedings on the Aircraft and Shipbuilding Industries Bill, the consideration of the application thereto of any Standing Order relating to Private Business be dispensed with."

The purpose of the motion was to enable the Bill to pass its remaining stages in the House of Commons as a public Bill. The House makes its own rules of procedure and can if it wishes in a case such as this choose to depart from its own rules, provided a majority of the House is in favour – though in fact the proposed departure in this case from Standing Orders relating to private business, an expression which would include a hybrid Bill, was without precedent. This statement aroused the collective fury of the Opposition, whose members began to shout in chorus, "Cheat, cheat!" From then on the debate was acrimonious and members on both sides of the House were constantly raising points of order.

Nationalisation of the two industries was obviously an ideological aim of the Labour government. Michael Foot's statement seeking to justify the motion on the ground that the jobs and livelihood of employees would otherwise be at risk was disingenuous and lacking justification. So far as the aircraft industry was concerned, it was certainly true that for both HSA and BAC, government contracts for the manufacture of military aircraft were a significant part of their businesses, but that state of affairs would have continued without nationalisation and did in fact continue years later after privatisation. In neither case were government contracts a form of public subsidy or charity, as Michael Foot's statement might be taken to imply. Contrary to any suggestion that nationalisation was necessary to protect jobs, there were good grounds to show that it was likely to result in redundancies for some parts of the workforce. Nationalisation in the form proposed in the Bill obviously involved the merger of the two main aircraft manufacturers,

HSA and BAC, and such a merger must inevitably involve losses of jobs. Both companies had Head Offices in which jobs would be duplicated on a merger, which would therefore result in redundancies. In my own case I was conscious that I had an opposite number in BAC, a lawyer who was on the company's board, so I had reasonable grounds for apprehension that nationalisation might mean dismissal because of redundancy. Furthermore, rationalisation following a merger would probably result in the closure of surplus production capacity. Indeed, the rationale of such mergers, whether achieved by nationalisation or by the usual machinery of one company taking over another, must be to achieve greater efficiencies and economies of scale. For the shipbuilding industry, the Bill also involved the setting up of a single corporation, British Shipbuilders, to take over the various private companies being nationalised. This being the case it would be reasonable to assume that the same process of rationalisation following a merger would take place and result in job losses. There was no proper factual basis for maintaining that nationalisation was a necessary step for saving the jobs and livelihood of people employed in these two industries.

The House moved on to other business and I left to go home. I had a ticket to attend the debate on the government motion the following evening, but decided that my attendance would not be worthwhile, as all the argument would be about parliamentary procedure and there would be nothing of substantive interest from the point of view of the companies being nationalised. I have always regretted my decision not to go back to the House of Commons the following night, because it meant that I missed witnessing a historic occasion and scenes of great excitement. The account which follows is therefore not based on personal experience, but as it was the most dramatic event in the parliamentary history of the Aircraft and Shipbuilding Industries Act and possibly the most dramatic event in the House of Commons in the second half of the twentieth century, it is worth recording at second hand. I am indebted to the relevant pages of *Hansard* for 27 May 1976, and to Michael Crick's biography of Michael Heseltine, published in 1997.

The business of the House, as explained earlier, was consideration of the motion for treating the Bill as a public Bill, notwithstanding the Speaker's ruling that it was hybrid. However, the opposition had put down an amendment in support of the ruling. As was to be expected, it was a fraught and acrimonious debate. The government regarded it as vital that the Bill should continue its progress towards enactment while the Conservative opposition clearly thought that the attempt to have the motion passed by the House would mean that proper parliamentary procedure was being overridden in the interests of achieving the ideological goal of nationalisation. The debate continued for four hours, with many points of order. A vote was taken shortly before 10pm. At that time the government had a very narrow majority in the House and the vote on the amendment produced the most unusual result of a tie, 303 in favour and 303 against. The House had to divide again and the Speaker had to exercise his casting vote, a very rare occurrence. By precedent the Speaker said that his vote had to go against the Opposition amendment and this time the amendment was defeated by 304 votes to 303. The main motion was carried. I quote Michael Crick's biography, page 189:

'As Labour MPs taunted the opposition front bench, it emerged that they had won only because a government whip had broken his "pair". The whip had made a traditional pairing arrangement with a Tory MP whereby both men had agreed not to go through the lobbies that night, thereby cancelling each other out. He should not have been voting at all.'

Government MPs, including Neil Kinnock, began singing the Red Flag in triumph. This was a red flag to a bull so far as Michael Heseltine was concerned, so in his anger he picked up the mace from the table between the two front benches. I again quote Michael Crick:

> 'The mace is nothing less than the symbol of the Crown's authority delegated to the House, and Heseltine now advanced with it towards the singing Labour members. If that was the respect they had for parliamentary democracy, he suggested, they might as well take the mace. MPs from both sides were horrified. Heseltine's front bench colleague Jim Prior quickly intervened.'

Prior grabbed the mace from Heseltine, put it back on the table and told the latter to get out of the Chamber, which he did. In spite of this, pandemonium continued and there were scuffles between opposing members. The sergeant-at-arms had to be called to help restore order and the Speaker adjourned the sitting. Heseltine later had to apologise to the House for his behaviour.

Trade Unions and Nationalisation

The commitment to nationalisation of the aircraft and shipbuilding industries was included in the Labour manifesto before the 1974 General Election. A consultative document on the programme for nationalisation was published by Tony Benn, Secretary of State for Industry, in January 1975. One item included in this document was a statement that the two new corporations would be used as guinea pigs for experiments in industrial democracy, and a provision to give effect to this was included in the Bill, though no attempt was made to define what the words meant. I have referred above to a madcap proposal for an extreme form of industrial democracy which was put forward by Tony Benn but happily was rejected by the then Prime Minister, Harold Wilson.

It was always apparent throughout the saga of

nationalisation, from statements made by ministers in parliament and elsewhere, that the trade unions were an important driving force. In the debates to which I have referred arising from the Speaker's finding that the Bill was *prima facie* hybrid, government ministers mentioned that the unions representing the workforce of the shipbuilding industry in particular had sent in telegrams expressing their concern about possible delays to the progress of nationalisation. During the consultation phase it became common knowledge that Tony Benn was much more interested in talking to trade union representatives than to the boards or senior managers of the companies involved. I recall hearing about a party of union representatives from one of HSA's factories who were invited to meet Tony Benn at his office and who were appalled that while they were given tea in proper cups and saucers, Tony Benn, true to his demotic ideals of inverted snobbery, insisted on drinking his tea from a mug.

One of the features of the aircraft industry at the time was the very high ratio of members of staff to shop floor workers, because of the large numbers of people employed in research, design, marketing, negotiating contracts, buying, product support and other activities. For the most part staff were not unionised. Copies of the government's consultative document were published widely and it occurred to many staff members that they needed to do something urgently to make sure that the opportunity which the document gave them to express their views on the future of the industry was not allowed to go by default. It was obviously necessary and desirable that their views should be expressed collectively, and to this end informal staff committees were improvised at the various establishments of HSA and BAC. I was responsible for calling a meeting of the staff of HSA's Head Office early in February 1975, with the full knowledge and approval of the company's General Manager. By this time I had been promoted to the status of Executive

Director Legal, a courtesy title for senior managers just below board level, so my involvement in consultations with staff employees generally began to look a little questionable and did in fact give rise to critical remarks by opposition Members of Parliament. Accusations were made that British Aerospace Staffs Association or BASA, the formation of which is described later in this chapter and of which I became the first chairman, was in fact what was derisively called at the time 'a sweetheart union', one that was favoured by management, not inclined to be at odds with management in any way and not independent. My position, combining a senior management appointment with the chairmanship of a staff union, obviously laid me open to this kind of attack, however unjustified it might be.

Consultation Rights Denied

The government introduced the Aircraft and Shipbuilding Industries Bill into the House of Commons in April 1975. This was the first of three attempts to get the Bill enacted, and on this occasion it was already so late in the session that the Bill did not progress beyond first reading. It was however, the signal for more intensive activity on the part of the work force whose members were going to be affected by it. It provided for the setting up of British Aerospace and British Shipbuilders as the two corporations which would take over the assets and employees of the companies being taken into state ownership. It imposed a vague obligation on both corporations to further industrial democracy, a concept which was much in vogue at the time and which the Bill did not define. One of its clauses required the corporations to carry out periodic reviews of their affairs for the purpose of establishing how their businesses should best be organised. The Bill eventually was enacted as the Aircraft and Shipbuilding Industries Act 1977. Section 7 of the Act, repeating provisions which had appeared in the various versions of the Bill, stated:

*It shall be the duty of each Corporation, **after consulting any relevant trade union** [emphasis supplied] to formulate in each year... a corporate plan relating to the conduct... of the operations of the Corporation... dealing... with the following matters:*

a. *capital investment*
b. *research and development*
c. *employment of persons*
d. *forecasts of income and expenditure on profit and loss account and of payments and receipts of the Corporation*
e. *such other matters as the Corporation considers appropriate, and*
f. *such other matters as the Secretary of State may... specify in writing to the Corporation.*

'Relevant trade union' was defined in the Act as 'any independent trade union, as defined in section 30(1) of the Trade Union and Labour Relations Act 1974 which the Corporation... recognises for the purpose of collective bargaining...'

'Independent trade union' as defined in the 1974 Act meant 'a trade union which was not under the domination or control of an employer'.

A previous nationalisation statute, the Iron and Steel Act 1967, under which the British Steel Corporation was established, had imposed on that corporation an obligation in similar circumstances to consult with *organisations of workers –* an expression not defined in the Act – *appearing to it to represent substantial numbers of persons in its employ.* The definition of 'relevant trade union' quoted above might sound neutral and unobjectionable, but when compared with the corresponding definition of organisations of workers in the 1967 Act, was obviously intended to impose major restrictions on the categories of employees who would enjoy consultation rights after nationalisation, and it became apparent that the intention was to limit those rights to members of TUC-affiliated trade unions. Such a limitation was clearly ideologically slanted and was certainly not compatible with the general notion of industrial democracy, a notion which by a separate section of the Act the two corporations were given a statutory duty to foster. The annual corporate plan would be an important management event but the Act by its restricted definition of those entitled to consultation rights excluded the large numbers of employees who were not members of independent trade unions. These were the middle managers, the designers, engineers, salesmen, accountants, negotiators of contracts as well as secretaries, clerks and other junior staff members, the kind of people on whom the proper functioning of any company depends. The definition in section 7 of the Act of the items which had to be included in each corporation's annual plan made it clear that consultation rights were of vital importance. Even if such employees formed their own trade unions they would still have to clear the hurdle of satisfying the Certification Officer, responsible under the 1974 Act for registering trade unions, that their unions were genuinely independent of the employers.

Moves Toward Forming a Union

As the political and legislative juggernaut taking the aircraft industry in particular towards public ownership continued to make progress, concerns among the industry's middle managers and others destined to having to accept an underprivileged status under the new regime grew. Contacts were made between the committees set up in the various establishments of the companies being nationalised and a national committee was formed. I was the only lawyer on the committee and became in effect its chairman, although at this stage we did not have any formal constitution or have the power to elect officers. I was largely responsible for drafting representations on the government's consultation document and later on the Bill, seeking in particular to have the restrictions on consultation rights removed so that such rights would be conferred on all employees.

Even at this early stage I was conscious that there was a certain incongruity about a senior manager with the title of Executive Director Legal engaging in quasi-trade union activities. But I never felt that there was any conflict between my obligations as the company's legal adviser and my unofficial role in assisting this important category of employees to articulate their views about a major upheaval of the industry which would affect the future careers and prospects of all of us. We were in no sense opposed to our employers, indeed we made common cause with them in seeking to have the Bill improved. I was of course simultaneously advising the Board of HSA on the detail of the Bill and suggesting ways in which the company ought to try to have it amended. The Board was just as interested as we were as individual employees in wanting the industry to be managed after nationalisation by a genuinely autonomous corporation and in wanting all employees to have equal rights to be consulted on important matters. As a matter of courtesy I kept the directors of HSA informed of what was going on. They did not attempt to influence or discourage me in any way and generally wished me well in this endeavour.

It became apparent to us from our contacts with politicians that the government would not relent or make any kind of concession to meet our concerns about denial of consultation rights. Those of us who were actively involved in dealings with government began to realise that we might have to think seriously about forming a union, not a notion which would readily appeal to many middle managers. The realisation grew however, that without the protection of our own union we might well after nationalisation be in the position of being the people in the middle, excluded from important consultations and negotiations between top management and shop stewards representing shop floor workers.

The Almondsbury Conference

Rolls Royce, the aero engine manufacturers, had been perforce taken into public ownership as a matter of national necessity by Ted Heath's Conservative government in 1971, following the company's financial collapse. The company's Bristol Division had had a successful management union for some time and this union issued an invitation to the committees which had by now been formed to represent the interests of middle managers and others in the factories and offices of the aircraft manufacturing companies slated for nationalisation for the purpose of considering the formation of a national aerospace management staff trade union. Invitations were accepted also by Westland Helicopters, Ferranti and other companies which supplied equipment for aircraft. The conference was held in July 1975 at Almondsbury, near the M4/M5 interchange.

It was taken for granted that any union we formed would not be affiliated to the TUC, for the following main reasons:

1. We felt that we needed a body concerned exclusively with the aerospace industry. Most TUC unions then had membership based on particular occupations with no special interest in any one industry.
2. TUC unions had political links with the Labour Party which would be anathema to many potential members of an industry union.
3. Many potential members would be professional engineers or belong to other professional bodies. It was felt that TUC unions did not understand the conflict which might arise for such people between orders from a union to take industrial action and the rules of their professional bodies. A union established specifically for looking after the interests of such professional people would be able to frame its rules

and conduct its relations with employers in such a way as to ensure that such conflicts were avoided.

This was a well attended and productive one-day conference. After much discussion the decision was taken that we should set about forming a management/staff association which would seek to be recognised and registered as an independent trade union as defined in the Trade Unions and Labour Relations Act 1974 and thus achieve consultation rights with British Aerospace after nationalisation. There was present at the conference the Chairman of the recently formed Shipbuilding Management Association. Representatives of staff and management of that industry, which was to be taken into public ownership under the same Bill, had already formed a union for the same reasons which had now led us to take this decision. Sharing this experience helped us greatly and we were able to obtain a copy of their rules. Being the only lawyer present at the conference, I volunteered to write the rules of the new union and the Rules of the Shipbuilding Industry's Association were of considerable help.

Drafting the Rules

Drafting the Rules was a considerable undertaking. We went through several drafts and several more meetings before we reached a form agreed by all involved. The union was to be called the British Aerospace Staffs Association (BASA), membership to be open to all staff of the companies being nationalised. The word 'staff' was not defined. This was a deficiency, but it was appreciated that there might be difficulties and anomalies in any attempt at a definition which would have to be suitable as a basis for recruiting members at the various establishments; we felt that a search for greater certainty would create problems and be illusory. In order to qualify as an independent trade union as defined in the 1974 Act the Rules made it clear that BASA would not be under the domination or control of any employer and not be liable to interference which might lead to such control. For the same reason the Rules had to state that calling for industrial action on the part of some or all of its members was within BASA's powers, though it was clearly understood by everyone at the outset that BASA was not formed for this purpose or for the purpose of negotiating with employers on salaries and other conditions of service. We had to take account of the problem of members who were bound by codes of professional conduct and a rule provided that such members were not to be subject to disciplinary action on account of refusal to take part in industrial action if by so doing they would be in breach of their codes.

Formation of BASA

We decided to go ahead with the formation of BASA in early 1976. Even at this stage, after many meetings and much correspondence, some of the site representatives were apprehensive on account of possible hostile reaction of TUC unions at their sites. Although the ground had been gone over many times at previous meetings, there were still those who were not sure that we were doing the right thing and who at the eleventh hour were counselling against formation of a union, expressing a preference for being satisfied with maintaining the loose links which we had established through our national liaison committee. In attempting to assuage such concerns we had always agreed that we would not seek to recruit members in sections of the industry's work force where other unions were already well entrenched.

A Formation Committee was elected to manage BASA's affairs pending the election of a National Council. I was elected as the first Chairman along with others including a General

Secretary and a Treasurer. All sites in the United Kingdom at which there was an expectation of forming a branch in due course were represented on the Formation Committee. Unfortunately, the staff groups at the factories of BAC and HSA in Lancashire and on Humberside felt unable to join. At HSA's factories in Manchester union pressure was exerted in an unpleasant fashion. There were some 700 potential members who wished to hold a meeting on company premises to discuss whether or not they should participate in the formation of BASA. At first the local General Manager agreed, but the local representative of the AUEW, the main engineering union representing shop floor workers, threatened to call a strike if the meeting were held, whereupon the General Manager withdrew his agreement. I later met the same General Manager, who accused me of stirring up trouble with the AUEW and other TUC unions. I tried to explain to him the motivation which had led to the formation of BASA. We had no quarrel with our employers but faced the prospect of becoming the employees of a state corporation which would not by law be under any obligation to consult us on vital matters as an important segment of the work force unless we were represented by an independent trade union. I asked him whether he expected us all to lie down in front of the TUC steamroller. All this he brushed aside.

I occasionally had meetings with personnel managers (this was before the now common usage of 'human resources' rather than 'personnel' became fashionable) who were hostile to BASA because of the effects that its formation and recruitment of members from the hitherto non-unionised part of the work force could be expected to have on relations with existing recognised unions. This was an understandable but worrying reaction. Management would obviously wish to maintain good relations with its workforce and avoid disruption caused by industrial disputes. But it is surely also in the interests of good management to accept the desirability of giving senior staff the right to join and be represented by unions of their own choice. At this time, the 1970s, unions were all powerful and capable in some cases of causing much damage to major industries. I quote the following from a report which I wrote at the time:

> *'If management does not support the establishment of staff associations, this may well result in closed shop agreements with TUC unions being forced upon them. Such agreements are now given every encouragement by the Trade Union and Labour Relations Act 1974 and there has been no shortage of cases of individuals who have refused to join a union which has a closed shop employer with the union being dismissed and finding themselves with no redress.'*

Trade unions now are constrained by a much tougher legal framework within which they have to operate than was the case then, and no longer have the same clout with private sector employers.

My Own Position and Resignation

In spite of all the support and sympathetic understanding which my being Chairman of BASA evoked from most if not all the members of the HSA board, I was always conscious of the potential conflicts between this appointment and my position as the company's principal legal adviser. In both capacities I was having to deal with legal questions arising out of impending nationalisation and sometimes had difficulty in remembering which hat I was supposed to be wearing. I fully expected that at some stage I could be faced with a serious personal conflict and in fact this happened at a much earlier stage than I had expected. Less than six months after we had formed BASA, I was summoned by the company's Director and General Manager, Eric Rubython, to his office. As he put it to me: "Your branch of BASA at Hamble [on the south coast] has approached the General Manager at Hamble and asked for recognition. In your capacity as Executive Director Legal, what do you advise that the company's response should be?" My reply was that his question faced me with a personal conflict of interests and necessitated my immediate resignation from the chairmanship of BASA. I went back to my own office and asked a senior purchasing manager who worked in the same building to come and see me. I told him of my conversation with the General Manager and asked him whether he would be prepared to take over from me as Chairman, subject to the approval of BASA's managing committee. To my great relief he immediately agreed and the formalities of my resignation and his appointment as my successor were soon concluded.

I left HSA in November 1976, to take up my appointment as Company Secretary of Wellcome, so my connections with BASA ceased entirely. I was informed later that BASA under its new chairman succeeded in achieving recognition and certification as an independent union. This would have entitled BASA to rights of consultation after nationalisation, but I do not know to what extent those rights were in fact exercised.

Conclusions

The experiences which I have described in this chapter left me with a very pessimistic view of the way the policies of an extremely left-wing Labour government were being directed toward turning Britain into an irreversibly socialist state in the 1970s. The prime movers were Tony Benn and Michael Foot. I have mentioned the former's happily unsuccessful attempt to foist an absurd form of industrial democracy on the aircraft industry and the latter's unfounded assertion in the House of Commons that the jobs and livelihoods of employees in that industry and also in shipbuilding depended on nationalisation going ahead. Another reason for pessimism was the hostile attitude taken by government and by Labour MPs towards the concerns expressed by the staff members for whose benefit BASA was established about the form that nationalisation was going to take and the unwillingness to concede consultation rights. At one stage while the Bill was going through Committee, BASA arranged a delegation jointly with the Council of Engineering Institutes, concerned with the future standing of professional engineers in the industry, to meet Gerald Kaufman, Minister of State for Industry and now Father of the House of Commons, who led for the government in piloting the Bill through Committee. We found him obdurate and unsympathetic. He told us that the limitation of consultation rights to relevant trade unions as expressed in the Bill was in line with government policy on industrial relations generally and had been insisted on by the Department of Employment. His attitude was one of hostility, which seemed to ignore the fact that by this stage we had a considerable membership and occupied collectively many vital jobs on which the success and prosperity of the industry depended. A Conservative MP who accompanied us to this meeting commented afterwards that the Minister seemed not to be taking into account in the way that he antagonised us the fact that we all had votes and that some of us might actually be Labour sympathisers whom by this attitude he was alienating.

This was a time when the trade unions seemed to be invincible. Ted Heath's government had caused the Industrial Relations Act 1971 to be enacted, a bold attempt to reform the anarchic world of industrial relations. The Labour government which was returned to office after the 1974 General Election had as a major priority the repeal of that Act, and section 1 of the Trade Union and Labour Relations Act 1974 boldly stated that the 1971 Act was repealed. There was a detectable mood of pessimism among the Conservative MPs whom I met during

157

the Committee stage of the Bill; a feeling that they were having to concede ground to a Labour government and could see no foreseeable prospect of ever recovering that ground. It took Margaret Thatcher and a robust policy of privatisation of state owned industries to reverse this trend and dispel the gloom.

During all this time I continued to work at HSA's Head Office in Kingston and was aware of a general feeling of dejection among my colleagues. We knew that nationalisation was going to happen but sadly there were no cheering messages from the board and there were no grounds for feeling optimistic about the future. During 1975, I started to wonder what sort of future I or others like me might expect and I even went so far as to apply for a job with a company in Canada. I actually went to Canada for an interview, to which I have referred in my opening chapter under the heading of '*Job Hunting*', but happily for me as it turned out, my application was unsuccessful.

IMMIGRATION APPEALS

I retired from my last job in full-time employment as Company Secretary of Wellcome at the end of October 1992, when I was 62. I began preparations for keeping myself occupied in retirement by being interviewed at the end of 1991 for an appointment as a part-time immigration adjudicator – a position which is now styled more appropriately as immigration judge. I was responding to a press advertisement which my wife Megan, ever a genius at finding jobs for me, had spotted. I was interviewed by Mark Patey, Chief Adjudicator at the time, whom I had known thirty-seven years earlier as a fellow member of the Devonshire Course at London University, run for training newly recruited cadet members of the Colonial Service. He had spent his years abroad in Swaziland. He was accompanied as interviewer by a young woman civil servant who irritated me somewhat. She knew from the CV which I had submitted in support of my application that I had had a very varied career in various posts of increasing seniority in manufacturing industry and commented in a supercilious manner, "You seem to be very product oriented." This clearly was the viewpoint of a mandarin looking down with disdain from the rarefied heights of a medium-ranking civil servant in the Lord Chancellor's Department (now the Ministry of Justice) at a lowly toiler in the sweatshops. I pointed out that even those working in the grubby surroundings of factories and offices had to deal with people. I could have been positively rude and reminded her that it was the wealth created by industry that produced the taxes that paid her salary, but refrained. I was appointed in early 1992, and began the training and first sittings as an immigration adjudicator which coincided with my final months as Wellcome's Company Secretary.

Immigration decisions are taken by Home Office civil servants either as immigration officers dealing with applications to enter the UK or as what are known as entry clearance officers at British diplomatic missions abroad. They deal with applications from countries outside the European Economic Area for visas as visitors, workers, students, persons joining family members who are already here or wishing to enter as spouses or fiancé(e)s of persons resident in the UK. In taking decisions they are required to follow a vast and complex body of Immigration Rules made under the Immigration Act 1971 and constantly being amended. Nationals of EEA countries are not required to have visas but enter the UK in exercise of Treaty rights and are subject to a different immigration regime under various EU Directives. Applicants for visas whose applications are refused in many cases have a right of appeal to a tribunal established for the purpose presided over by lawyers appointed by the Ministry of Justice with the modern title of immigration judges. Nowadays, this is an extensive jurisdiction with some hundreds of full and part-time immigration judges sitting in London, Birmingham, Glasgow, Manchester, Leeds and other provincial cities, disposing of thousands of appeals a year. There are no wigs, gowns or other ceremonial trappings, but the procedure is much the same as that of an ordinary civil court.

My previous judicial experience was that of an Assistant District Commissioner sitting as Magistrate in Sierra Leone between 1954 and 1959, and I took to my new appointment very quickly. Many of the appellants who brought their cases before me were from Asian and African countries and my past years first in Sierra Leone then later in India, meant that I could readily relate to the physical and cultural backgrounds relevant to their cases. Sometimes indeed I had before me appellants from India or Sierra Leone.

The Jobs That Never Were

Once I started sitting as an immigration adjudicator I became aware that some of my fellow part-time judicial colleagues had similar jobs sitting to hear appeals in Social Security Tribunals. The option of having two part-time judicial appointments in different jurisdictions had a certain appeal and I asked the officials of the Lord Chancellor's Department (now the Ministry of Justice) whether I could be considered for another job to run concurrently with the one I already had. The LCD had nothing to offer at the time, but I was invited to contact the Ministry of Agriculture and Fisheries, which was in the process of setting up a new statutory tribunal, the Sea Fish Licensing Tribunal. Legislation had been passed for the purpose of restricting fishing boats to a limited number of days at sea annually, so as to conserve fishing stocks. My recollection is that the legislation also provided for compensating the owners of vessels from public funds if the allocated ration of days at sea caused hardship. I never became familiar with the detail of the Act of Parliament in question, for reasons which will become apparent.

I applied successfully for an appointment. The job of a tribunal judge was to hear appeals against allegedly unfair decisions of the actual Authority. The Minister responsible had promised in the course of debate in Parliament that the sittings of the tribunal would be held at the relevant fishing ports, which meant that they could sit at any fishing port in the United Kingdom. When applying, apart from giving all the usual details required in a CV I had said that I would be happy to travel to any fishing port for the purpose of hearing appeals. This might have meant visits in the middle of winter to such delightful spots as Grimsby or Fleetwood. After a lifetime of job hunting I had the unique experience of being offered and accepting a job without being interviewed for it. I received an appointment letter from the Secretary of the Tribunal, along with copies of official publications on North Sea fisheries, explaining the problem of declining fish stocks and what the government was hoping to achieve by introducing the system of days at sea quotas. But the system had to be ignominiously abandoned by the government before it started because the trawlermen took a leaf out of their French counterparts' book and began to engage in collective protests by blockading harbours.

In 1993, the government of Gibraltar advertised a vacancy as an Additional Judge and although I had by this time retired from being Company Secretary of Wellcome and had started hearing appeals as an Immigration Adjudicator, I could not resist the temptation of applying. I was invited in June of that year to travel to Gibraltar for interview. I have to admit that this was only a month after Megan and I had moved house from Surrey to our present abode in Great Bedwyn near Marlborough. Megan has always supported me in my career moves and indeed on several important occasions has drawn my attention to advertisements for posts for which I then successfully applied. On this occasion however, she had very understandable concerns that if I got the job it would mean a move to Gibraltar when we were still settling down in Wiltshire.

The procedure adopted for interviewing applicants was unusual, in that all six candidates, one of whom was like me a part-time immigration adjudicator, were invited to travel on the same plane, stay at the same hotel (all at government expense of course) and all invited on the morning after our arrival to assemble in the Chief Justice's court to meet the Chief Justice, Alastair Kneller, later knighted and as it happened a contemporary of mine from Corpus Christi College Cambridge. Gibraltar is a very small colony of around 30,000 inhabitants, so the Chief Justice was in fact the only judge of the Gibraltar Supreme Court. In spite of its minuscule size the colony has the full apparatus of colonial government with governor, deputy governor, administrative secretary, Attorney General, Commissioner of Income Tax, Chief of Police, magistrate etc. It has long been internally self-governing so it also has a chief minister and cabinet. As part of the planned programme each of the candidates for the post had a brief meeting with the Governor. I had the distinct impression that His Excellency did not have much work to do, hardly surprising as all executive authority was vested in the local cabinet assisted by an ample retinue of civil servants. I guess that the governor's functions were mainly ceremonial.

The decision to appoint an additional judge had been taken because Gibraltar was seeking to compete with Bermuda, the Channel Islands and other dependent territories to attract companies by offering a tax haven, which could be expected to give rise to some commercial litigation. The appointment would be for three years and would not be pensionable, but a lump sum payment would be made at the end. I was aware of Megan's concerns but nevertheless felt that it was an appealing prospect, the warmer climate being an important part of the attraction. I had an interview with the Deputy Governor and asked whether it would be practical to live just over the border in Spain and commute into Gibraltar, where space is limited. The answer was a firm no. As part of the price to be paid for admission to the European Union (or European Economic Community as it was at the time) the Spanish government had had to agree to open the border between La Linea and Gibraltar, which had been firmly closed for some years. However, the Spaniards were determined to continue showing their displeasure at continued British sovereignty by making border crossing slow and inconvenient. This meant that every vehicle entering Spain had to be searched, allegedly for contraband cigarettes, so cars might have to wait for over an hour to cross.

So the fortunate person appointed to the position would have to accept probably rather cramped accommodation in Gibraltar. Apart from this, there was only one courtroom, normally used by the Chief Justice. Pending provision of something better, the additional judge would have to hold court in a sweaty law library. Anyhow, much to Megan's relief, I did not get the job and neither did any of the other five candidates. Someone else was appointed and sadly died not long after taking up the post.

Asylum Appeals

During my ten years as an adjudicator there was a huge increase in the numbers of asylum applications from people arriving in the UK by various means, sometimes illegal entrants. Such applications have to be considered under the United Nations 1951 Refugee Convention to which the UK and most other countries are parties. For an application to succeed the applicant is required to show that if he is returned to his country of origin there is a reasonable degree of likelihood that he will be at risk of persecution, meaning that his life or freedom will be threatened on account of his race, religion, nationality, membership of a particular social group or political opinion. This is not a very exacting requirement of proof but nevertheless most applicants fail, either because their story is not believable or if it is it falls short of showing a risk of persecution. Most failed applicants appeal and perhaps 20% of appeals succeed. In my time I heard some 600 asylum appeals and allowed about thirty. Some of the appeals which I dismissed were then taken to a higher appellate level, but very few succeeded at that level.

From time to time people whom I have told about my experience with asylum appeals have said that I must have heard some heart rending stories. My reply to that is that I did, but I rarely believed them. Hearing the evidence in all these cases made me extremely cynical about the readiness of people to tell blatant lies in pursuit of their own ends.

The following is a summary of my best remembered case. An appellant who was clearly a Pakistani gangster first appeared in court before me handcuffed to a prison warder. He was getting towards the end of a five-year prison term for manslaughter of an individual in the United Kingdom. He had fled Pakistan some years previously after committing a murder for which he had been tried and convicted in his absence. On appeal to me he produced in evidence a hotel bill from one of the Gulf States which purported to show that he was there and not in Pakistan on the date of the murder. The bill had not been produced to the court in Pakistan and it was apparent to me that it was a forgery. He pleaded that the judgment of the court which convicted him and sentenced him to death was politically motivated and wholly unjust. However, the Home Office submitted in evidence a copy of the Pakistani court's judgment (no juries there) setting out in English, still in practice Pakistan's main official language, the powerful evidence against the man supporting his conviction. There was no other evidence to support the plea of political motivation. It was very clear that he had a criminal record in Pakistan, had fled the country in order to avoid arrest for murder and become involved with criminal gangs after arriving in the United Kingdom.

Before I disposed of and dismissed the appeal the man finished his sentence for manslaughter but was immediately arrested and detained under Immigration Act powers. He appeared again in my court and his lawyer applied for bail. All the court rooms had places at the back for members of the public, friends and relations, but they were normally occupied only by two or three people at most. The hearing of this bail application was different. There were about twenty people who had turned up in support of the appellant, evidently influential members of the local Pakistani community. It could have been a bit intimidating for me but they behaved respectfully. One man who was their spokesman said that they were prepared to put up bail for as much as £250,000 and I had the strong impression that he and his companions had the wealth necessary to make such an offer. As the conventional requirement of bail in such cases was £2000 this made it clear that the appellant was someone special in his community. However, I refused bail for good reason. Some years previously Asil Nadir, a prominent businessman facing trial on fraud charges and bailed in large sums had fled to North Cyprus in order to escape justice (he returned to the UK later voluntarily but was tried, convicted and is now serving a prison sentence); so *a fortiori* as lawyers say, the appellant before me would have an even stronger incentive to abscond rather than be deported to Pakistan where he faced the death penalty. My decision was calmly accepted without protest. I later dismissed the appeal and had no further involvement in the case but heard much to my surprise that the unsuccessful appellant had returned voluntarily to Pakistan.

Lack of credibility was the main reason for dismissing asylum appeals. The adjudicator hearing an appeal always had with him the Home Office file on the appellant's case, including the complete record of what he had told the interviewing case worker in support of his application. Often the appellant would tell the court a completely different story and destroy his own case. To be a successful liar in such a case you need to have a very clear memory of what you said before and a ready facility for invention. Few people are thus gifted. However, it was apparent in some cases that the appellant intentionally told a different story; the reasoning seemed to be that he had failed with the story told to the Home Office so he had better try his luck with a different and better story on appeal – but of course in doing so he dug an even deeper hole for himself.

Apart from the kind of case mentioned in the previous paragraph these are some of the reasons for not believing the appellant:

- The appellant took a long time before leaving his own country. He alleges that he was tortured, imprisoned and otherwise persecuted but nevertheless remained in the country for months or even years carrying on a normal life before deciding that he needed to leave for his own safety.

- Long delay in claiming asylum. For example, it is common for people who come to the UK on a six-month visa to claim when the six months have almost expired.
- Clearly opportunist claims. It is very common for illegal immigrants, who may have been in the UK for years in some cases, to claim asylum when they are arrested (e.g. in raids on Indian restaurants). Illegal immigrants can be deported or removed, but not so asylum seekers whose cases are pending.
- A seriously unbelievable story, otherwise the fairy godmother syndrome. Such stories were often told because the appellant wanted to disguise the evidence of the often unlawful means by which he had entered the United Kingdom. As one example of many, a Tamil from Sri Lanka gave evidence that he was brought to the UK by an agent who travelled with him. The agent took him to Kennington Underground station and left him there, saying that the appellant should wait and he, the agent, would shortly be back. The agent never returned, but the Tamil claimed that he was saved by another Tamil who just happened to be on the spot, noticed him there and immediately invited him to go to his home and enjoy free board and lodging indefinitely. The most likely truth was that the Tamil already resident here had arranged with his countryman in Sri Lanka (who might well have been a close relative) to smuggle the latter into the UK.

It is a lamentable fact that most asylum seekers are not genuine but are economic migrants making bogus asylum claims as a means of enabling themselves to remain in the United Kingdom.

Other Appeals

Forced marriage is recognised as a social evil which is still prevalent in some ethnic communities in the UK. The

Immigration Rule which governs the grant of visas allowing a foreign spouse to come to the UK on marriage, imposes two particularly important requirements which have to be met, namely that the parties to the marriage have met and that 'each of the parties intends to live permanently with the other as his or her spouse and the marriage is subsisting'. I have always construed this as meaning that the marriage should be a genuine one and that there should not have been any family coercion on the spouse living in the UK. Usually, appeals against refusal of such visas were made on behalf of men in the Indian sub-continent and were supported by evidence given by wives or fiancées living here who would normally be accompanied in court by their parents, very much involved in organising the marriage. Even if the woman came alone she would still be under parental influence and if her evidence failed to bring about a successful appeal would incur the wrath of the parents, which in some cases led to her murder, a so called 'honour killing' at the hand of her own parents or other close relatives. Sometimes the only way such women can survive is to escape from the parental home and hide in special refuges set up for them by voluntary organisations. These were difficult cases.

One unusual case which came before me was an appeal by a woman living in India against refusal of a marriage visa to enable her to join her husband in the UK. He was a well educated and articulate young man earning a good salary in employment as an accountant but even so had had to give in to pressure from his family to go with them to India and go through a ceremony of marriage with the woman. As soon as he returned home he fired off a series of faxed messages to the entry clearance officer in India making it very clear in no uncertain terms that he did not wish to have the woman join him in the UK and would refuse to accept any responsibility for her if she came. Inevitably, the visa application was refused. I read the file with all these messages on it before the hearing and was mystified as to what possible basis there could be for any appeal against refusal. At the hearing the young man was asked by his counsel what was his reaction when the application was refused and he replied, "I was shocked" to which I could not forbear saying, "Do you really expect me to believe that?" The evidence which he gave in support of his appeal was that when he sent off these messages he was having an affair with another woman, very much under her influence and not responsible for his own actions. I did not believe this either, but even if it had been true I would still have had to dismiss the appeal as it was very apparent from the man's actions that the marriage did not meet the requirement of the Immigration Rules that the appellant and her husband intended to live together in the UK as man and wife.

I recall another case in which the appellant was a man still in India and the wife came to the hearing as sponsor, accompanied by a friend but without her parents. She made it clear that she had been pressed into the marriage by her parents and did not want the husband to join her. In the normal way this should have been recorded by me as evidence and the basis for dismissing the appeal. However, we were wary in such cases of the possible consequences which the sponsor could face, which might be as drastic as murder. I therefore dismissed the appeal without quoting her statement and said that she had been present but had chosen not to say anything. Even so, as I later heard, she was in serious trouble with her family.

Sometimes, there were rather sad cases brought by Thai or Filipina women appealing against refusal of marriage visas to enable them to join their British husbands in the United Kingdom. The men were usually middle aged lonely bachelors, divorcees or widowers, who had been working as expatriate employees of oil companies, airlines or other organisations in the Middle East or South East Asia and had met much younger women who were very ready to marry them and thereby be able to move to the United Kingdom and enjoy a much higher and more prosperous standard of living than in their home countries. The man would normally come to the hearing as sponsor of his wife's appeal and I was rarely in doubt in his case that so far as he was concerned it was a genuine marriage. The woman was still in her own country and I had to form a view as to how genuine she was from letters sent to the man and other evidence to show that her affection for him was genuine – a delicate and sometimes embarrassing exercise of prying into the intimate details of a marriage. In such cases it was difficult to overcome a natural bias in favour of a native Briton, middle class as well as middle aged, and obviously desperate to avoid declining years of loneliness. But the Immigration Rules had to be applied just as strictly in these cases as in any others and I often had to conclude that disparity in age, cultural and linguistic differences, and above all absence of persuasive evidence of any real love or affection on the woman's side meant that the appeal must be dismissed. A few years after I had retired from hearing immigration appeals Megan and I met on holiday in Switzerland just such a couple as one of those whose cases I had in the past had to consider. He was a retired lawyer aged about 60 and she was a Thai woman in her late twenties who could speak some English but was far from fluent. There was not much apparent communication between the two of them and little evidence to indicate that they were a happy couple. The man admitted in conversation that his wife spent a lot of time on the telephone to her family in Thailand and made frequent trips on her own back to Thailand to visit them. I felt sorry for both of them.

The Lighter Side

Hearing and determining asylum and other appeals was a serious business with not many laughs, but two entertaining incidents in my experience are worth retailing. Both relate to applications for bail on behalf of immigrants detained under Immigration

Act powers while their cases were under consideration. In the first one I was hearing the application in court and would have been prepared to grant it. I would have needed proof from the surety of ability to stand bail for £4000. The young lawyer conducting the application said that the prospective surety had a bank balance of that amount and produced a bank statement in support. The statement did indeed show a figure of £4000 but it was a *debit* balance in red ink on a mortgage loan account – a detail which the lawyer had failed to notice.

The other application in a different case was made by a letter from the applicant's solicitor. It was quite a long letter and in the course of it what she obviously meant to say was: 'My client has been incarcerated for some time which has been detrimental to his health.' What she wrote however was: 'My client has been *incastrated* for some time etc.' Well, of course that would have been detrimental to the poor chap's health.

I had to take the late John Mortimer QC to task for serious inaccuracies in his short story '*Rumpole and the Asylum Seekers*'. In this story Rumpole takes on an asylum seeker as a client in an appeal against Home Office refusal and represents him at a hearing before a tribunal. Apart from making it clear in general terms that he had no idea how these cases were dealt with, Mortimer committed two howlers in his use of terminology. The Home Office was represented at hearings by a Home Office Presenting Officer, who in the story became a Home Office *Presentation* Officer. Much worse than this was that the tribunal chairman referred to the Presenting Officer as a 'Prosecutor'. This was completely out of place as an asylum or immigration appeal is not a criminal proceeding and no one is being prosecuted for anything. I wrote to Mortimer to point out his errors and he replied admitting that he had never had any experience of immigration or asylum appeals – which he had made fairly obvious. I felt that his failure to do a bit of basic research before writing this story was particularly unfortunate. Rumpole became a famous fictitious criminal advocate and obviously when writing about Rumpole's cases at the Old Bailey or other Crown Courts Mortimer was drawing on his own considerable experience as an eminent QC with years at the Criminal Bar. His readers naturally assume that the detail of Rumpole's appearances in court or in chambers represents authentically what goes on in the real world. Sadly, some of his readers may have erroneously taken it for granted that his account of the conduct of an asylum appeal as described in this short story was likewise reliable.

Migration Watch

In 2002, at the age of 72, having reached the statutory retirement age for judges, I was obliged to retire from being a part-time immigration adjudicator and accepted an invitation from Sir Andrew Green (ennobled in 2015 as Lord Green of Deddington), Chairman of Migration Watch, now a well-established and respected think tank, to become its Honorary Legal Advisor, a position which I continue to hold. Over the years I have endeavoured to keep pace with the rapid and voluminous changes in immigration law, have attended monthly meetings of Migration Watch's Executive and have contributed a large number of legal briefing papers to its website. I take pride and pleasure in this continued activity.

NOW IT CAN BE TOLD

No one will be surprised if I now admit that when writing *Remote Corners* fifty-two years ago in India, describing my then recent experiences as an Assistant District Commissioner in Sierra Leone, I left out some events which were not to my credit. I am now very happy to lift the censorship on the most egregious of these events.

My confession relates to the period when I was Assistant District Commissioner in Kambia District in 1957 and 1958. We were expecting a formal Governor's visit, always a major event in a colony and a fraught affair which involved a great deal of preparatory work. The Governor's aide de camp (ADC), who normally had to look after the Governor in Freetown and everywhere else, organising his household and office and taking care of all the minutiae of a Governor's day-to-day official life, was a contemporary of mine, Eric Fisher. Eric's father had just died and he had gone home at short notice to attend the funeral. As a consequence the Governor was due to arrive in Kambia minus ADC, and I was drafted into the job. He arrived in the Governor's barge *Cara* from Freetown, coming up the Great Scarcies River and landing at the wharf in Kambia.

As soon as he arrived we began discussing with him plans for his stay. Eric Fisher's sudden departure meant that not all the preliminary preparations had been completed. There was to be a cocktail party for a large number of local notables on the first evening on the lawn of the District Commissioner's house and a dinner party in the house, (which the Governor took over for his stay), on the second. Lists of those who were to attend these two functions were settled and it fell to me to arrange the completion and despatch of invitations. I got clerks in the office working at filling in the cards and messengers to take them post-haste to the invitees. All this happened on the morning of the cocktail party.

Mike and Helen Sandercock, the temporarily dispossessed DC and his wife, were perforce lodging with me while Sir Maurice and Lady Dorman occupied their house. I went back to my house at about 4pm and was met by Mike who pointed out to me that the dinner party invitations had been issued bearing the same date as that for the cocktail party. Fortunately, all but one of the invitees for dinner were in Kambia and could be quickly informed of the error. But there was one guest, Dennis Garvie, a Scots engineer in charge of an irrigation project, who was based at Rokupr, twelve miles away. I obviously had to act quickly to try to warn him of the mistake. We had no telephones or other quick means of communication in Kambia. I therefore wrote out a note and gave it to a messenger whom I sent off in one of the Governor's Land Rovers to try to get it to Garvie, who would be setting off from Rokupr in black tie and dinner jacket, inappropriate wear for a cocktail party, and which would draw attention to the fact that he had been invited to a dinner party to which most of the guests at the cocktail party had *not* been invited – most embarrassing. The messenger did not however know Garvie and the two vehicles passed each other on the road, going in opposite directions. Garvie arrived in Kambia where he was intercepted by Mike and told of the mix-up. Fortunately, he was a pleasantly humoured person who took it well and simply set off back to Rokupr forthwith, foregoing attendance at the cocktail party. This event went ahead and I was there in attendance, feeling terrible about the cock-up for which I was responsible. In accordance with protocol, when the time came for the guests to leave, I asked Helen as senior lady present to lead the way, which she did dutifully.

As soon as all the guests had left I had to face His Excellency and tell him the awful truth. Sir Maurice was a tall and impressive figure and I felt minute and miserable standing before him making my confession. When I had done so he said, "I will apologise to Garvie," to which I replied, "Sir, I must apologise, it was entirely my fault." Sir Maurice then responded in regal fashion, "Mitchell, it was *my* invitation, *I* will apologise." His final dismissal was, "Mitchell, I realise you are doing this job on the hop, but do remember if you ever have to work for me again, no detail is too small to overlook." I wanted the earth to open and swallow me. Happily, all the other arrangements which I had to make in the course of the visit went well and after Sir Maurice returned to Freetown he sent me a handwritten letter thanking me for all my work as his temporary ADC and for the efficient way in which I had performed my duties.

I felt duly chastened, made my personal apology to Garvie, and was fortunate that he was of an equable and forgiving disposition. I suppose I could excuse the error I had made on the ground that everything was being done in haste and I might be forgiven for my failure to check everything as I ought to have done.

TOO OLD TO LEARN?

During my final years of full-time employment, the predominant climate in Wellcome, and probably in most other organisations was in favour of early retirement and the general thinking was to the effect that anyone over 60 was necessarily past his or her best. I always felt that my responsibilities as Company Secretary were such as to warrant my appointment to the Board and I raised this twice with my bosses; first with Chairman and Chief Executive Sir Alfred Shepperd when I was just over 50 and a second time with his successor John Robb, when he had just taken over as Chief Executive and I was 60. I had more responsibility, measured by headcount of staff under me and size of budget, than at least one of the directors. I was responsible for sixty staff, mainly lawyers and other professional people as well as secretaries and other administrative and clerical staff. In my last year in the post I controlled a budget of £13 million. It was by no means unusual in major companies for the Secretary to be on the Board. I put these arguments as forcefully as I could on both occasions but with no success. John Robb in particular was adamant that he was not going to have a 60-year-old being appointed to the Board.

Immigration law

My experience since retirement from full time employment at the age of 62 strongly gives the lie to the myth that people over 60 are past their best and incapable of tackling anything new. In my last year with Wellcome I took up an appointment as a part-time immigration adjudicator (in modern parlance an immigration judge), which I continued to hold until I was 72 and was perforce retired under the statutory provision on judicial retirement age. I have given an account of my experience in this field in a separate chapter. My previous experience of holding judicial office was as an *ex officio* magistrate in Sierra Leone between 1954 and 1959. I had no previous acquaintance with immigration law, which in any case became ever more complex during my tenure of office with the passage of four substantial Acts of Parliament on asylum and immigration plus the Human Rights Act 1998, an enactment which has much relevance to cases on immigration and asylum law. I take some pride in having mastered the job well during my ten years, having had very few of my determinations (the approved word for the judgements we had to write when deciding cases) overturned on appeal and having continued since my retirement from it to keep my interest in this field of law alive and useful in my capacity as Honorary Legal Adviser to Migration Watch, now a highly respected think tank concerned with levels of immigration into the United Kingdom, and chaired by Lord Green of Deddington, former ambassador to Saudi Arabia.

One aspect of working as a lawyer in industry which I greatly enjoyed was the sheer variety of legal experience which it required: company law, contract, employment, some familiarity with tax law and with areas of law of particular concern to the company which employed me. I had ten years with Hawker Siddeley and sixteen years with Wellcome, so I had to be familiar with areas of the law affecting the design, manufacture and operation of aircraft at first, then with the complex legislation regulating research and development, manufacture, advertising and selling pharmaceutical products. In both companies, product liability was of major concern, deaths of injury in the one case caused by aviation accidents and in the second case caused to patients by defective or allegedly defective medical products. Both companies were internationally active; Hawker Siddeley by exporting and Wellcome by both exporting and trading through a large network of subsidiaries and associated companies worldwide. This meant that I had to become acquainted with at least some relevant aspects of the laws of the countries in which both companies were trading, usually consulting local lawyers as necessary. But I have for the last twenty-four years, from the time of my retirement, become a specialist in immigration law, having been very much a general commercial and international lawyer for most of my working life before that. Indeed, immigration law is the only area of the law in which I can claim to have specialised.

Social housing

I take pride also in having entered the field of social housing in 1994 and becoming Chairman of Sarsen Housing Association shortly before it took over the social housing stock of Kennet District Council, our local authority based in Devizes at the time. We had been living in the district for a little over two years and I had no previous familiarity with the complexities of social housing, still less of all the elaborate tasks which had to be undertaken in setting up a new association from scratch and organising its financing, staffing and management. I had had experience of being Chairman of various committees but this was a responsibility of a very different order. Sarsen started with 5000 properties, housing a significant proportion of the district's population. We established a loan facility with the Bank of Scotland and other banks of £120 million and during my years as Chairman drew down £60 million to pay for the transfer of stock. I continued as Chairman until 2001, and at my own request was able to stand down and hand over to Vice Chairman John Heffer, but remain on the Board. The Chief

Executive, Terry McColl, worked well with me and we had an excellent relationship, although we had little in common between us. I had spent my life for the most part working first as a colonial civil servant and then as a lawyer in industry and my main interest outside work was and is music. He had spent his working life as a housing manager in local government and his hobby was vintage cars. Sadly, he died suddenly in November 2001, shortly after John Heffer had taken over the chairmanship. I was very happy to continue as just a plain Board member, but I became frustrated over the next few years at the increasing bureaucracy over which I now had no control, so I happily obeyed a standing order which said that no one should continue as a board member past the age of 75 – although no one was pressing me to go and I am sure that I could have continued indefinitely had I so wished. So I had my third retirement in November 2006, shortly after my 76th birthday. A minor drawback was that until 2003, it was not possible to pay Board members and there was much impassioned argument within the housing association movement as to whether payment should be made possible. Even when it was finally allowed, a few years before I retired, the fees were and area on a very modest scale.

As Chairman of Sarsen Housing Association I was called upon on two occasions to greet the Princess Royal at opening ceremonies for new developments. The first such occasion was in November 1996, in Tidworth, a garrison town in Wiltshire. We had bought several blocks of apartments from the army and refurbished them for occupation as social housing units. The Princess had accepted an invitation to come and ceremonially launch the project by unveiling a plaque. The event was to take place one evening in the ground floor of one of the apartment blocks. I was in charge as chairman and I arranged for a welcoming line of Sarsen's Chief Executive and local authority councillors and officials, all of us with spouses. The Princess arrived, driving her own Rolls Royce. I was there to meet her as she stepped out of the car and was presented to her by the Lord Lieutenant of Wiltshire who was with her. This was required by royal protocol, though the Lord Lieutenant and I had never previously met each other. I began to introduce by name the people standing in line but the Princess moved along the line shaking hands with everyone at such a pace that I could not keep pace with my introductions. The next bit of the proceedings was to introduce the Princess to a married couple who were the first tenants and had already occupied the main apartment on the ground floor. The chairman of the Association's housing committee was supposed to be waiting at the entrance to the apartment for this purpose, but in fact she had gone inside, so I had to ring the bell so that the Princess could be admitted – a trifle embarrassing. However, after these slight contretemps all went well, the plaque was unveiled, a couple of speeches were made and some food and drink was provided for the Princess and her ladies in waiting, the lord lieutenant, councillors and local authority staff, as well as board members and managers of the housing association.

I was greatly impressed by my conversations with the Princess. I could not describe her as charming but she obviously takes her duties seriously and was well informed on the subject of social housing – in some ways better informed than I was.

My second meeting with the Princess was in June 1999, again at a formal opening ceremony, this time at a major new development in Devizes. Sarsen had acquired the local mental asylum, no longer used for its original purpose, for conversion into a housing estate, mainly social housing but including a number of properties for private letting. The asylum consisted of a group of solid nineteenth-century buildings. Included in this volume is a photograph of the Princess with myself and a young mother tenant at the door of one of the properties. I had learned my lesson from the previous occasion and there was no line up of notables to be presented. I introduced the Princess just to our Chief Executive and to the Site Manager of the contractors who had been doing most of the work on the conversion.

On thinking further about my time as Chairman of Sarsen, it seems to me not unreasonable to describe it as the best job I ever had, even though it was unpaid. My reason for saying that is that I was the boss of a sizable organisation, but not answerable to anyone. Sarsen owned 5000 properties at the time, had 120 employees headed by a very efficient Chief Executive, and a turnover of several million pounds annually. I was of course as Chairman accountable to the Housing Corporation, at that time regulator of social housing, but I was able to take a fairly independent line and not take lying down unfair criticisms which sometimes came my way. In all previous occupations which provided me with a living, from being an Assistant District Commissioner in Sierra Leone, to being Company Secretary of Wellcome, I always had a boss and many of the bosses were difficult and sometimes unpleasant people. At Sarsen I was spared all that and had the pleasure of heading a substantial and well-managed association.

Computers

Computing is another area where I have built up my skill since retirement. As Wellcome's Company Secretary I had a terminal on my desk for my last two years and learned to make some use of it. However, I was still diffident about taking the major step of acquiring my own hardware. In any case, the internet was in its infancy and emails had not yet been invented. I have to give credit to Roger Sashaw, my daughter Kamini's second and now divorced husband, for having helped me to get started. He was a major in the Canadian Army, seconded to the British Army at Lulworth from 1997 to 2000, and had built up a considerable amount of computer expertise. He helped to identify what kit I needed to get myself started, ordered it for me and installed it all when it arrived. At first I was learning by trial and error and finding it most frustrating. However, I persevered and became more proficient. A computing course which I attended in Marlborough in 2000 was a great help and I became fairly competent in Microsoft Word and Excel. I have continued to add to my skill and would now feel seriously bereft without my computer. I have not attempted to become familiar with the workings of social media, so although I am aware of Twitter and Facebook, I do not attempt to use them. A friend enrolled me in LinkedIn, a most inappropriate organisation for me, as its purpose is to act as a means of younger people furthering their careers by advertising themselves and making themselves known to possible employers or other contacts. Megan and I both have mobile phones which we do not normally have switched on, but take with us when we are away from home for use in emergencies.

Music

Another area is music, the subject of the next chapter, a lifelong passion from the age of fourteen, on which I have spent far more time than before since retirement.

MUSIC AND LANGUAGES

German

My three main intellectual passions in life have been languages, music and the law. My natural aptitude for languages became apparent when I started to learn French at Darwen Grammar School. To this was soon added German in special classes for which the headmaster, Hector Gaskell, was the teacher and which were held in the headmaster's study on Saturday mornings. The favoured pupils were a select bunch who had shown a fair degree of competence at, and enthusiasm for, languages. One of the others was the late Bill Coupe, with whom I struck up a firm friendship and who later became professor of German at Reading University. A distinctive feature of Hector Gaskell's teaching was that of learning German through songs. I can still recall and sing the words of most of the songs I learned, 'Die Lorelei', 'Heidenröslein', 'In einem kühlen Grunde', 'Das Wandern ist des Müllers Lust' from Schubert's *Die schöne Müllerin*, and many others. By comparison, from French lessons I can recall 'Frère Jacques' and that bloodthirsty national anthem 'La Marseillaise' and not much else.

Hector Gaskell was a remarkable man, a classical scholar who had married a German wife and become fluent in the language. With his German wife he was a most energetic headmaster of Darwen Grammar School throughout the war. In 1945, almost at the end of the war, he was appointed headmaster of another public school and for Bill Coupe and myself this meant a major upheaval. There was no other German teacher on the staff and arrangements were made for both of us to move to

Bolton School in about May 1945. This was a major change and without it my life would have been very different and I am sure much less varied and exciting than it has turned out.

Bolton School had a higher standing in the educational hierarchy than Darwen Grammar School. Although it was not a boarding school it had the status of a public school as the headmaster was a member of the Headmasters' Conference. It was well endowed by William Hesketh Lever, the founder of Unilever. It was a boys' school though there was a separate girls' school in an adjacent building. Moving there meant for me and for Bill Coupe, a daily journey to Bolton by train.

Music

The important aspect of the move for the purposes of this chapter was that my musical education began in earnest. The school had its own orchestra and choir and gave a concert of high standard every year. Also, soon after the move to Bolton, I began piano lessons. We had moved to a bigger house and my father bought a second hand grand piano on which I began to learn. Fourteen is rather a late age to begin learning to play a musical instrument, but I was eager to learn and made rapid progress. Before long I joined the school choir, initially as a tenor but later as a bass. I never learned to play an orchestral instrument, so was unable to join the school orchestra. I had already begun to attend symphony concerts locally, mostly in Blackburn, where the Hallé and the Liverpool Philharmonic Orchestra were regular visitors. I became familiar with Beethoven's symphonies and other standard classics. My first experience of opera was a performance of La Bohème at a theatre in Bolton by the Carl Rosa Touring Opera Company. The great feature of Bolton was that I was able to enjoy the company of boys who were also enthusiastic about music and from whom I could learn a lot. There was at least one outstanding pianist, Irving Wardle, who at one school concert played Chopin's Revolutionary Study and at another the first movement of Beethoven's last piano sonata, Opus 111 – neither of which I have ever been able to manage with any success. There was also a brilliant organist, Keith Bond, who became an ARCO at the age of sixteen. Within a year of starting to learn the piano I had made friends with Keith Pemberton, later a contemporary at Cambridge, and we began to play piano duets. I also became friendly with a violinist and with him played a Grieg piano and violin sonata in F, Opus 8. In June 1948, I was judged to be competent enough to play a piano solo at the school concert and chose the second of Debussy's two Arabesques. Later in the year I took part in music performed on Speech Day and played Schubert's Impromptu in E flat, Opus 90 number 2. Looking back on this I am astonished at my audacity in playing in public and from memory a work dominated by continuous high speed running passages – more or less perpetual motion. I would certainly not attempt anything so bold now, but I was making the most of the energy and enthusiasm of youth.

I have to acknowledge the benefit and enjoyment I obtained from music lessons in the Sixth Form at Bolton. I never took any examinations in the subject, but those of us who had an interest had two periods a week under the music teacher, Percy Stevens. I recall vividly three of these lessons in which works of Beethoven were analysed, the Pathétique Sonata, the Violin Concerto and the Seventh Symphony, named by Wagner the apotheosis of the dance. From the first I learned to understand the elements of sonata form and I can truthfully say of all three lessons that I have remembered their content all these years in much more detail and with much more pleasure than any of the hundreds of other lessons in many different subjects which I sat through in the course of my education. We also did a certain amount of unison singing in these classes and I extended my acquaintance with the Lieder repertoire, notably learning Schubert's setting of Goethe's 'Erlkönig' and Schumann's 'Die beiden Grenadiere'. The words, the settings and the piano accompaniments of both remain completely familiar to me to this day.

For the last eighteen months or so before I was called up for national service in February 1949, I was the pupil of my father's brother, Uncle Walter. He had trained as a professional pianist at the Northern School of Music in Manchester, but had never succeeded in his ambition to make a career in music. He made a living by managing the Mitchell family business but so far as I could judge was never happy in it. He had two children of his own, a boy, John, and girl, Frances, but neither of them had ever shown any interest in music, so he welcomed me as a keen nephew and pupil. I had previously learned the basics from another teacher, but the real progress I made in improving my technique and becoming better acquainted with the piano repertoire was gained from my uncle as teacher. Towards the end of my time as his pupil he wanted me to learn to play the final movement of Beethoven's Moonlight Sonata, a virtuoso piece calling for much playing of arpeggios at high speed. I regret to say that I never made it and am resigned to accepting now that so far as I am concerned it is unplayable.

Perhaps that particular objective might have been achieved, but on 21 February 1949 I had to report for national service in the RAF, so that for a while meant a break in the progress of my musical education. In the course of national service I seldom had access to a piano.

However, I spent over a year in Germany and was able to take advantage of the opera houses in Lübeck, my first posting, and Göttingen, where I spent most of the time. In Lübeck, I heard *Tannhäuser*, my first experience of Wagner on stage. It was probably not a particularly outstanding production, but I was bowled over by it. In Göttingen, I lived in a requisitioned house at 81 Herzberger Landstraße, perhaps the smartest residential area of the city, just a short walk from the opera house. Here I became acquainted with Verdi, with productions of *Aida* and *Un ballo in maschera*. I also went to productions of works other than opera, and having acquired a reasonable degree of fluency in German, I enjoyed Lehar's *The Merry Widow* and Goethe's poetic drama *Torquato Tasso*, as well as occasional performances of German cabaret. On Sunday evenings, I often attended symphony concerts. I guess that the variety of cultural entertainment was at least in part due to Göttingen being a well-established older university town. On one occasion I was able to attend a lecture delivered in English in the University Aula by T.S. Eliot, then at the height of his fame as a poet. I regret to say that I have no recollection of what the lecture was about.

I went up to Cambridge to begin my first year in October 1950, immediately after the end of national service. I joined one of the university's music societies, which gave me access to the various piano practice rooms in the music school. Keith Pemberton, my duet partner from Bolton, came up to the same college at the same time and we sometimes went to the music school to play duets, or even on occasion, two-piano music. In our second year, 1951 to 1952, we arranged to share a suite of rooms, a common sitting room and two separate bedrooms, and hired a piano for the year. We played duets by Schubert, Mozart and Dvořák, mainly for our own entertainment. The college had its own music society which organised intimate chamber concerts in the Master's Lodge on occasional Sunday nights in term time. At one of these concerts we played one of Dvořák's Slavonic Dances, Opus 46.

The college had rules about the hours during which playing of musical instruments was forbidden. The sitting room which Keith and I shared was directly over the Senior Combination Room. One day at about 3pm, I was happily playing, unaware that there was a meeting of Fellows in progress in the room below. I was soon made aware of it by a visit from the Dean of College, Dr Harley Mason, and had to desist. I apologised for my transgression and did not have to face any further disciplinary action. I have recorded in the chapter on sport my regrets at not having devoted more time to music while up at Cambridge and having instead pursued the mistaken activity of rowing.

As preparation for going to Sierra Leone to take up my appointment in the Colonial Service, I was for one academic year, 1953-54, a student in London on the Devonshire Course, run to train Colonial Service cadets. I lived for that year in a British Council hostel at 1 Hans Crescent, London, SW1 – a very good address just next door but one to Harrods – which was mainly a home for students from the colonies who were pursuing a variety of courses in London. There was some music and I took part in the choir formed by residents and by friends of residents. Before Christmas 1953, I was asked by one of my colleagues on the Devonshire Course to organise some Christmas carols with the intention of singing them in some of the wards at Guy's Hospital. My experience of choral singing was limited and I had never trained a choir, but I accepted the responsibility. We managed to find enough sopranos, altos, tenors and basses to form a passable choir, and some of them were experienced choristers. My recollection is that we mainly rehearsed *a cappella* and one of the men obligingly brought along a recorder to give us the notes to get started. It was a reasonably successful venture, much appreciated by the patients and nurses, and we were entertained afterwards to coffee and mince pies by the matron.

Sierra Leone offered nothing in the way of musical life and the realisation that service in most colonies meant enduring a dearth of music was one of the reasons why I was a reluctant recruit. I had access to a piano just twice in my years there, once in the European club in Bo and once when I was a guest of American missionaries in Mattru in Bonthe District. The missionaries were pleased to have someone who could accompany them in singing some of their hymns. One of the problems with having a piano would be that of tuning in a hot and humid climate where frequent tuning would have been necessary. Nowadays a solution for that sort of climate would be a combination of air conditioning and an electronic piano which never needs tuning. The former was becoming available to the more prosperous expatriates, but I doubt whether electronic pianos had been invented in the 1950s. In any event, I had to manage without electricity for more than half my time in Sierra Leone. Music in Sierra Leone meant for the most part native singing and drumming, West Indian calypso music for the more sophisticated locals and European dance or other light music for the expatriates. Occasionally, I heard reasonably good performances by the Sierra Leone Police Band and they were particularly skilled at the routine of 'Beating the Retreat'. I have always found the 'Sunset Call' on the bugles with which it ends very moving.

I have a memory of a rare treat one evening in Bo when a friend of mine played a recording of *Così fan tutte*. On leave I was able to go to concerts and opera performances in London or Manchester. On my second leave in 1958, I was able to borrow a piano which was installed at my mother's home in Darwen and was pleased to find that in spite of having hardly touched a piano for the previous four years I had not forgotten how to play and could still manage passable performances of items such as Mozart minuets with which I was already familiar.

In India, for the first time in my life I had the enjoyment of family life in a home of my own, although it was of course not my own property but a bungalow in a compound for which I paid rent. I was able to rent a piano in Bombay and have it tuned from time to time. I spent many happy hours getting to know Beethoven's sonatas and much other music. Had we lived in Bombay it would have been possible to find other musicians with whom to join, but at a distance of twenty miles in the middle of an industrial suburb that was impractical. Apart from the piano I had bought a record player which we took out to India with us, along with a small selection of classical LPs. There were occasional concerts of classical music in Bombay and Megan and I were able to hear a recital given by Yehudi Menuhin, accompanied on the piano by his sister, and on another occasion a piano recital by Shura Cherkassky. He played in the Cowasji Jehangir Hall, a dignified venue endowed by and named after a wealthy Parsee. Unfortunately, it was not air conditioned, so it was a bit sweaty and I felt sorry for the pianist in his formal white tie and tails. There was the continuous background noise of the ceiling fans whirling and the twittering of a number of birds which seemed to live in the roof of the hall. There was also a symphony concert performed in the open air in a sports stadium, conducted by Malcolm Sargent. There was a major demonstration going on nearby and the demonstrators marched past the stadium shouting their slogans to the accompaniment of the music.

On our return to the United Kingdom in January 1964, there was another two-year gap without a piano until early 1966, after we had moved from our house in Hereford to the house in Molesey, Surrey, where we lived for the next twenty-eight years. I bought a good second-hand upright and began to make up for lost time by resuming playing in the leisure time I had from commuting to and working in London and spending time with the family. In the early 1980s, when I was beginning to feel moderately prosperous, I spent £2000 on buying a Zimmermann baby grand piano, which I still have. In Molesey, a close neighbour was a young professional pianist whom I had the pleasure of acquainting with the piano duet repertoire, with which he had not previously been familiar.

Living close to London meant that it was possible to take advantage of the concerts and opera performances, which we did. My London opera-going began with a performance of Wagner's *Die Meistersinger von Nürnberg* at the Coliseum in 1968, followed by plenty of other visits. After I moved to Wellcome as Company

Secretary in 1976, I was able on occasion to go to the opera at the company's expense. The company had four seats in the stalls at Covent Garden every Thursday night, which provided a ready means of entertaining business visitors, though sometimes they were available for private use by directors and other senior people. The company also supported Glyndebourne and from 1978 on, I enjoyed the privilege of an allocation of four tickets in the stalls once a year, again with the objective of being able to invite company guests. I usually invited lawyers, insurance or trademark experts who did work for the company. On two occasions my guests were the Uruguayan ambassador and his wife, he being a lawyer who had when in private practice in Uruguay looked after the interests of Wellcome's subsidiary company in the country. Since I retired in 1992, Megan and I have continued to go to Glyndebourne every year at our own expense and greatly enjoy the experience.

In May 1993, following retirement from Wellcome in October 1992, Megan and I moved to Great Bedwyn near Marlborough in Wiltshire, where we still live. Musically and in many other ways it proved to be an excellent move. The village has a music society which for more than twenty years has been putting on professional concerts at least four times a year. We also have an annual event called the Members' Concert, at which local keen amateur musicians perform and raise funds help to meet the costs of the professional concerts. Since 2011, I have had the pleasure and privilege of organising this event, which normally attracts a large audience and raises some hundreds of pounds for Music Society funds. I have now been retired from full-time employment for twenty-three years and although I have always managed to keep myself occupied to a great extent by taking part-time jobs and activities, have made good use of the extra leisure time which retirement affords in improving both my enjoyment of music and my personal participation in musical pursuits. As a consequence I have become familiar with an extensive repertoire of ensemble music, playing compositions by Beethoven, Mozart, Brahms,

Mendelssohn, Schubert, Schumann and other composers, piano duets, piano and violin sonatas, piano trios, and occasionally piano accompaniments for Schubert's Lieder and other songs.

For a number of years I went annually to a summer school for pianists which used to take place at the Royal National College for the Blind in Hereford. This was an event lasting a week which attracted enthusiastic and mostly very competent amateur pianists from all over the country to attend classes run by leading professional pianists. I attended the class for accompanists, at which a small number of instrumentalists and singers acted as guinea pigs, making themselves available to individual members of the class to play with them. The college was chosen as a venue because it provides training for blind people as piano tuners and technicians and in consequence has a large number of pianos in individual practice rooms, of which all of us made good use every day. The day was taken up with classes and private practice and every evening there was a concert of piano music performed in turn by the professional musicians who were tutors. Attending this class every year did much to improve my playing and I was later introduced to a professional teacher living in Basingstoke, Jean Murphy, a former concert pianist, to whom I went for tuition for several years.

Locally, I was introduced to a piano circle of about twenty enthusiastic amateur pianists living for the most part in or near Devizes. We met monthly at each other's homes and each played a piece which he or she would have rehearsed. There was plenty of knowledgeable discussion of the music played and of music generally. Sadly, the members were mostly over 70 and latterly numerous deaths brought about the demise of the circle. I did try to recruit some new, younger members to revive it, but had no success.

In 1999, an enterprising woman resident of the village decided to try to start a local choir, which became the Bedwyn Millennium Choir and still functions and prospers under that name. I joined from the start and briefly at the beginning acted as choir pianist. Our first public performance was on 1 January 2000, in the open air in the middle of the village. Happily, there was a clear blue sky and the weather was kind to us. Since then the choir has had its ups and downs but every year has continued to play its part in the village's musical life, singing carols at Christmas, having its own summer concert and taking a prominent part in the annual Members' Concert mentioned above. We normally have about thirty members and, as in the case of most amateur choirs, women are in the majority. We do not attempt anything too ambitious, no whole oratorios or anything on that scale, though we did in 2015, give a creditable performance in full of Fauré's 'Requiem'. We perform a wide range of religious and secular items and have achieved a good reputation locally, with the result that we are occasionally invited to perform at weddings and funerals.

Living in a Wiltshire village, with no concert hall or opera house within easy reach, means that keeping up with the contemporary world of music requires something of an effort. But we do make the effort and are not starved of music. Many years ago in the course of a job interview I was asked by the interviewer what different career I would have chosen if I had been free to make the choice. I had no hesitation in replying, "Being a musician."

My Personal Choice

This is my choice of music which I would favour if I were ever asked to be the guest on Michael Berkeley's Sunday lunchtime programme *Private Passions* on Radio 3 – not that there is any likelihood that that will ever happen. All these pieces have some personal association.

1. Kathleen Ferrier singing, in English, 'Che farò senza Euridice' from Gluck's Orpheus and Eurydice. This was

my mother's favourite piece of music and she would play a record of it over and over again.

2. The overture to *Tannhäuser* to mark my first experience of a live performance of Wagner in Lübeck.

3. Debussy's two Arabesques, the second of which I played as a piano solo at a school concert in 1948.

4. 'Moon River' sung by Audrey Hepburn accompanying herself on the guitar in the film *Breakfast at Tiffany's* at a party in New York, which Megan and I saw in Bombay and which we have since then regarded as our song. In Bombay we lived under a regime of alcoholic prohibition, though as foreign residents we were allowed a monthly alcohol ration. This had something of an inhibiting effect on social life in the expatriate community of Bombay in marked contrast to the lively party in the film.

5. The second movement, 'The March of the Pilgrims' from 'Harold in Italy' by Berlioz. In 1969, I twice visited Mexico on Hawker Siddeley's business. There were few direct flights then between London and Mexico City, so I made two of my four journeys by Air France, travelling via Paris. 1969 marked the centenary of the death of Berlioz and Air France provided a tape of Berlioz recordings including 'Symphonie Fantastique', 'Nuits d'été' and 'Harold in Italy'. I listened to these over and over and became and remain a devotee of Berlioz and particularly of the last named.

6. Beethoven – String quartet in B flat major, Opus 130, fifth movement Cavatina. A solemn and beautiful piece, long ago chosen by me as one of the desired items to be played at my funeral.

7. Strauss – 'Beim Schlafengehen', the third of his four last songs, the other piece of music chosen for my funeral.

8. Schubert's Fantasia in F Minor for piano duet D 940. A marvellous work written late in Schubert's short life, called a fantasia but in the form of a four-movement sonata with no breaks between the movements. The opening theme of the first movement returns in the final movement and

forms the basis of an elaborate fugue. The greatest of all piano duets, which Gill and I sometimes play.

9. The late Peter Maxwell Davies's "Orkney Wedding with Sunrise". This is a work from 1985 which Megan and I heard at what was possibly its first public performance at the Gleneagles Hotel in Scotland. It was played by the Scottish Chamber Orchestra, conducted by the composer, who lived for years on the Orkney Island of Hoy and explained the programme of the piece beforehand. It depicts the celebration of a wedding on an island on which, because of the loss of young people to emigration, weddings had become rare events. The wedding was followed by a boisterous party, with authentic sounding Scottish tunes of thecomposer's own invention. As the musicians and other revellers become more and more intoxicated, the music descends into organised chaos. Davies told us that he had been a guest at the wedding party which went on all night and he walked home in a brilliant sunrise. The master surprise stroke was that at the end of the work sunrise was represented by a piper in full Scots regalia who walked into the Gleneagles ballroom through the audience from the back of the ballroom in which the concert was held playing a tune which restored order from the chaos. It was a wonderful *coup de théâtre*. I was able to have a brief chat with Davies afterwards. I congratulated him on the piece and told him that I thought it would be very appropriate for the Last Night of the Proms. A few years later it was in fact included in the programme of the Last Night, complete with piper, but whether its inclusion resulted from my conversation with Davies I have no means of knowing.

DEFENCE OF BRITAIN'S IMPERIAL RECORD

I spent five years as an Assistant District Commissioner in Sierra Leone and recorded my experiences in *Remote Corners*. As a result of that experience I became persuaded that the British Empire was a great institution which made tremendous contributions in so many different ways to the creation of the modern world. I acknowledge that there were some parts of Britain's imperial history which are shameful and do not reflect any credit on the imperial power. It would indeed be remarkable if an empire which governed so many diverse parts of the world's surface and included within it so many millions of people of different races did not have some failings in parts of its record. But the imperial record has always had more than its fair share of detractors, particularly in the media and even more notably in the BBC. In recent years I have frequently been in correspondence with authors and others writing books or newspaper articles or making television programmes which appear to me to be very one sided and biased in the accounts which they give of colonial history. I have sought to correct ill informed or blatantly prejudiced statements and tried to educate the authors of these accounts to understand that they need to take a broader and less biased view of the subject.

Tim Butcher

Tim Butcher is an author and journalist who was born in 1967 and now lives in Cape Town, South Africa. Between 1990 and 2009 he was on the staff of *The Daily Telegraph* and among other appointments held during those years he was the newspaper's Africa Bureau Chief and Middle East Correspondent. In 2007, he published his first book *Blood River: A Journey to Africa's Broken Heart*, which is an account of a journey which he made in 2004, achieving the remarkable feat of crossing Africa from Tanzania to the mouth of the Congo, following more or less the route taken by HM Stanley, also a correspondent for the same newspaper, in the 1870s. *Blood River* describes what to most of us would seem to be an incredibly arduous, dangerous and for most practical purposes, impossible journey. The author describes how the infrastructure of a modern state created by the Belgians before independence in 1960 has disintegrated. The towns and cities through which he passed can no longer sustain modern civilised existence. Water and power supplies, telephones, railways and boat services on the River Congo have all simply ceased to function. Roads in and between major towns have deteriorated to such an extent that they are no longer motorable and have been reduced to tracks through the rainforest. A few aid workers and other relatively privileged people are still able to use motorcycles on them but for the most part the only communication is either on foot or by bicycle. On top of all this there has been a complete breakdown of law and order.

From time to time on his travels Tim came across one or two expatriates who somehow managed to survive amid the chaos and the dangers of the Congo, and the following passage quotes a Belgian woman living in Kalemie on Lake Tanganyika:

> "'I have got used to the lack of water. I have got used to the lack of power. I have got used to the lack of supplies in town. But the thing that makes today so bad is the lack of the rule of law. There was a time when at least there were some police who could keep some sort of order, or even soldiers you could go to, but today there is nothing.'"

Throughout the book Tim has nothing good to say about Belgian colonial rule. He regards it as having been brutal and exploitative. In places he acknowledges that the Congo was from 1880 to 1908 a personal fiefdom of King Leopold and few historians would question his harsh judgment on that period, but in 1908, the Belgian state took over responsibility for the territory and it became a Belgian colony. There are plenty of passages in the book which refer to the high quality infrastructure of a twentieth-century state, particularly its excellent communications. All this was of obvious benefit to the population as a whole and to a large extent must surely be taken into account when assessing the successes and failures of colonial rule. As an example of the deterioration of communications I quote the following passage from page 138:

'By 1949 the colonial authorities boasted 111,971 kilometres of road across the Congo. By 2004 [the year in which Tim crossed the Congo], I doubt if there were more than 1000 kilometres left in the entire country.'

In the final chapter, Tim describes a journey by Jeep from the capital Kinshasa to the main port of Matadi at the mouth of the River Congo. This was apparently in usable condition and presumably accounts for part of the 1000 kilometres mentioned in the quotation. It is obviously an important road but he notes that recent repairs had been paid for by foreign aid donors, a humbling state of affairs for the government of a country which has some of the world's richest reserves of valuable raw materials. He notes also that because the road was in better condition it had attracted the activities of numerous highway robbers.

For part of the journey, Tim was able to travel on a United Nations boat on the River Congo from Kisangani downstream. The commander of the boat was a Malaysian UN staff member called Ali who was particularly critical of the evident apathy of the local people and their failure to make the most of the natural advantages which the country provided. I quote the following account of the conversation between Ali and the author from page 309:

"'I don't know what it is about these Congolese people, or Africa in general, but look at this wasted opportunity," he said one morning… He pointed at the river bank, which at that point was crowded with palm trees, the remnants of an abandoned plantation producing palm oil.

"In Malaysia, people make millions from palm oil. It is one of the most valuable commodities in the world right now. It's used in the best lipsticks and cosmetics, it is used for all sorts of food preparation and it is even used to make fuel that is more environmentally friendly than petrol. There are businessmen in Malaysia who would give anything to get access to the palm plantations along this river.

"But the Congo people. They don't want to make money for themselves. They just want to take money from others."

I offered the standard explanation about the Congo's problems, that the Congo had suffered under colonialism and, when independence came, the Congo was pulled apart by forces beyond its control, as the Cold War preoccupations of the West allowed Mobutu, under American patronage, to run the country into the ground.

"That is rubbish," Ali said. During our trip I never saw him so animated. "Malaysia was colonised for centuries too, most recently by the British, a colonial rule that was cruel and racist. We got independence at roughly the same time as the Congo in the early 1960s, and we were even drawn into a Cold War conflict for year after year as communist insurgents fought for control of Malaysia. But somehow Malaysia got through it and the Congo did not. Today Malaysia is part of the rest of the world. People go on holiday in Malaysia. The world's business community does business in Malaysia. We even have a Grand Prix every year in Malaysia. The same is not true of the Congo. How can you explain the difference?"

He had distilled the quintessential problem of Africa that generations of academics, intellectuals and observers have danced around since the colonial powers withdrew. Why are Africans so bad at running Africa?'

The quotation ends with an important question, but Tim does not give an answer. I felt much aggrieved at some of the statements in *Blood River* and in March 2008 wrote to Tim at some length explaining my concerns. I was and still am lost in admiration for his fortitude in tackling such an arduous journey. It involved risks to personal security and health to a degree which put it on a par with the journeys undertaken by explorers in the nineteenth century. The journey was across the former Belgian Congo, but the author makes criticisms which he claims are just as applicable to the colonies of the other colonial powers. My complaint was that on the one hand he had nothing but ill to say of the record of the Belgians, but the dominant theme of the whole book is a lament for the deplorable state of the Congo now, more than fifty years after independence, by comparison with the highly efficient modern state it had been under Belgian rule. He does not actually refer to it as an efficient modern state, but that is a reasonable gloss to put on his frequent references to the functioning roads, railways, cities, etc. which used to exist and function and which by the time of his journey had almost completely crumbled and gone back to jungle. The main criticism which can be made of the Belgian record is that the Belgians did little or nothing to prepare their colony for independence, with the result that the event arrived with a rush and resultant chaos. They had not sought to emulate the progress made in British colonies in particular where steps were taken to create the conditions needed for functioning democracy and the creation of a cadre of African politicians and civil servants so that they could at least make a reasonable start in maintaining a civilised and functioning society after independence. But in spite of these shortcomings the Belgians had built a prosperous and well-run state for the benefit of the whole population, which to a large extent could be regarded as compensating them for the failure to obtain the benefits of democratic rule.

I quote the following passage from page 320 of *Blood River* in which the author talks of:

> '... the Congo I had traveled through, a country where I had seen human bones lying too thick on the ground to be given a decent burial; where a stranger like me was implored to adopt a child to save it from a life of disease, hunger and misery; **and where some people were so desperate they actually pined for the old and brutal order of Belgian colonial rule.'** [Emphasis supplied.]

Tim's reaction to my criticisms was robust and we had a frank exchange of views. In his response he said that his criticism of colonialism was that it was:

> 'predicated on the outsider knowing best over and above the local. From that basic inequality flowed so much, whether it was Belgian cruelty in nineteenth-century Congo, British torture in Kenya in the 1950s, French manipulation in the Ivory Coast in the 1970s (even though they were meant to have left as a colonial power a decade or so before), etc.'

I did not and do not now find anything in his reactions to my criticisms which causes me to change my basic view that in spite of many failings and errors the record of the European colonial powers in Africa is nothing to be ashamed of. Within the lifespan of a single individual, roughly between 1880 and 1960, they created the boundaries to which for the most part the independent states which they established have continued to adhere. They built roads, railways, schools and hospitals and established courts and police forces, all of which formed a valuable legacy which in the case of the British and French colonies created the foundations of modern states.

In spite of his initial reaction, Tim was keen to be friendly, wanted to bury the hatchet and expressed the hope that we might some time be able to meet over lunch, preferably before he started writing his next book, which was to be based on his overland travels through Sierra Leone and Liberia. In fact we did not meet until October 2010, by which time he had published his second book, *Chasing the Devil – The Search for Africa's Fighting Spirit*. In the travels described in this book he was following on foot more or less the same route as that taken by Graham Greene in 1935, recorded in *Journey Without Maps*. We met in late 2010, when he called to meet Megan and myself at our home in Wiltshire, when he was in the middle of a tour around the country promoting his second book. We discussed Africa for an hour or so before he had to be on his way, and I was sorry that the conversation could not have gone on longer. In the space of just over two years between our initial mildly acrimonious exchanges and this meeting, Tim had taken the trouble to buy and read a copy of my book, *Remote Corners*, and sent me some photographs he had taken in the Kono district in Sierra Leone, which had been my last posting before I left the country. He now lives in Cape Town, but I am hopeful that I might one day have another chance to have a longer conversation with him. In these paragraphs I have taken the liberty of referring to Tim by his first name on the strength of friendly acquaintance.

I have read *Chasing the Devil* which was of special interest to Megan and me because of our own experiences in Sierra Leone, admittedly now a long time ago. Once again I admire Tim's fortitude and endurance in undertaking a journey in often trying circumstances. I was pleased that in this book he does not appear to be particularly antagonistic to Britain's imperial record in Sierra Leone. I acknowledge as well as this book an article by Tim which appeared in *The Daily Telegraph* on 26 August 2010, entitled 'Henry

Morton Stanley was more hero than colonialist brute'. What gave rise to the article was a proposal to erect a statue of Stanley in Denbigh in North Wales, the town where he was born. Some critics had objected to the planned statue on the ground that it 'romanticised Victorian-era imperialists'. In making clear his disagreement with this view, Tim says, championing the fame and reputation of his distinguished predecessor as a correspondent of *The Daily Telegraph*:

> *'The Stanley I got to know through the journey and research does not deserve to be denied a modest statue because of blanket sensitivity about colonialism. If such political correctness were to ban honours for anyone who supported colonialism, then we would have to burn the books of Kipling and cast down likenesses of Churchill.'*

On the strength of these sentiments Tim might almost be regarded as an unrepentant imperialist, though I doubt that. In *Blood River*, Tim acknowledges the humanity and concerns that Stanley had for the surviving followers who had accompanied him across Africa in a journey which had lasted almost three years. When he finally reached the mouth of the Congo he made sure that passages were arranged for them all to return to Zanzibar from where they had started, and himself went with them, which delayed his return to the United Kingdom by several months.

As a matter of courtesy I sent a copy in draft of the foregoing paragraphs to Tim Butcher, who but for one minor change in the words, to which I readily agreed, was content for it to be published.

The BBC

In recent years the BBC has incurred much justifiable criticism for its left-wing bias, which goes contrary to the requirement in its charter to maintain balanced views. This has been noticeable in any programmes concerned with imperial history. There has been for example in recent years a series of programmes presented by Jeremy Paxman giving a distorted view of the history of British India, which did not even mention the early establishment of British rule by the East India Company. What follows is an account of my own vain efforts to challenge a thoroughly slanted view of the history of British African colonies.

On 15 August, 2012, BBC Two broadcast a programme called *The Last Explorers* an account of the life of David Livingstone, presented by Neil Oliver. It was well researched and insofar as it summarised Livingstone's life it appeared to be objective and factual. But at the end it turned into an anti-colonial tirade with the following remarks:

> *[Stage 1] Neil Oliver: But what followed was less attractive. Other European empires became interested in Africa, at least in part because explorers like Livingstone had mapped great swathes of it.*

> *The 'Scramble for Africa' was an opportunity, and also a ruse to throw tribal populations under the yoke and create a system of exploitation that was legal, but every bit as shameful as the slave trade. Livingstone's fame had drawn all of Europe's eyes to Africa. He'd made their maps for them. So it is altogether a blessing that he could not see the ugly future when he died that night in May 1873. That night, he could see what he had done and why he had done it, but not the consequences.*

I complained also about a further statement uttered against a background of happy Africans gathered in the evening in a village:

> *[Stage 2] Zambia was one of those new nations. By 1964, they were very glad indeed to be rid of the imperialist yoke. They celebrated.*

My complaint was about the lack of balance and distortion in these two statements, in the following terms:

Neil Oliver presented a well-researched programme on David Livingstone, but at the end of the programme he went off the rails by purporting to sum up the history of Africa in the twentieth century in just a few loaded words. He described the colonial experience of Africa as a period of exploitation and oppression, by implication a continuation of the slave trade, with no redeeming features such as bringing law and order or creating the infrastructure of modern states. He then referred to post-colonial Africa as a period of joyous liberty, ignoring such horrors as misrule by Idi Amin in Uganda or Mugabe in Zimbabwe, genocide in Rwanda, long running and lethal wars in Congo, perpetual chaos in Somalia, a destructive and bloody civil war in Sierra Leone, corruption and destruction of democratic institutions on a major scale. The record is grim. His remarks show breathtaking ignorance about Africa. I quote from the final paragraph of Martin Meredith's comprehensive and authoritative survey The State of Africa (2005):

'After decades of mismanagement and corruption, most African states have become hollowed out. They are no longer instruments capable of serving the public good. Indeed, far from being able to provide protection to their citizens, African governments and their vampire-like politicians who run them are regarded by the populations they rule as yet another burden they have to bear in the struggle for survival.'

The BBC's response was an exercise in self-serving and ignorant pedantry. In his first reply the Complaints Director insisted that the remarks of which I had complained referred only to the period of the Scramble for Africa, roughly between 1880 and 1914 and not to the whole period of colonial history. As I had unreasonably assumed that they did extend to the whole period, clearly my complaint was not justified. Then he said that 'it is a matter of record that colonisation in this period resulted in exploitation of peoples and natural resources of Africa' – in other words a record that could not possibly be disputed. In a second letter replying to my own comments on his first letter the Complaints Director insisted that the remarks in the programme could not be taken as referring to the whole period of colonial history as opposed to the limited period of the Scramble for Africa. 'Nothing in the text seems to me to lend itself towards your interpretation of it as encompassing a much wider timeframe and I do not agree that this is the meaning which viewers would have taken from it.' He did not believe that the remarks 'would have materially misled the audience on the colonial records of Britain or other European powers'.

The nearest I got to an acceptance that I might have a point in my complaints was an admission that 'the argument that this period was "as shameful as the slave trade" is debatable.' In the view of the Complaints Director the justification for this comparison with the slave trade was the fact that the colonial powers used forced labour. It is true that forced labour was a feature of colonial rule in some territories but it was a long way removed from any of the attributes of slavery. Even in Sierra Leone, where I worked in the 1950s, forced labour was required for clearing bush paths. Without it movement around the areas away from motor roads, which were maintained by paid labour, would have become eventually impossible. It was normal for young men to be required to work from time to time to clear the paths and this practice could reasonably be regarded as a form of tax paid in kind instead of in cash. Any attempts on the part of the chiefs to use forced labour to their own personal ends would have been strongly resisted and in some cases did result in riots. I should make it clear that forced labour in Sierra Leone was a matter of native customary law and it had no basis in legislation. So if I as an Assistant District Commissioner needed carriers for my baggage when visiting those parts of the district which did not have motorable roads, I would tell the local chief in advance and ask him to have carriers available. The young men would be there on the chief's orders and they would be paid by me for their labour.

As I was not satisfied with the responses I had had from the Complaints Director, I exercised my right to appeal to the BBC Trust. I pointed out that slavery meant the ownership of individuals and the denial to those individuals of all rights, including the right to life. Forced labour by contrast meant some restriction on freedoms and some relatively onerous obligations but otherwise the individuals concerned were at liberty to exercise rights of ownership over land and other property and to the protection of the law. It seemed to me that merely to admit that the comparison was 'debatable' was an outrageous understatement.

Dealing with the remarks identified as Stage 2 in paragraph 2 above, I said that although there was specific reference to Zambia, the clear intent was that end of colonial rule was a subject for continued celebration long after the event, not only in Zambia but in former colonies all over Africa.

I found no greater degree of enlightenment or understanding on appeal to the BBC Trust than I had found in my dealings with the Complaints Director. After I lodged the appeal I received from the Trust what purported to be an objective summary of exchanges between myself and the BBC and a summary of the Trust's own investigations into the issue. The investigation was set out as a synopsis of the history of colonialism in Africa in the nineteenth century with references to a number of sources. The acquisition of colonies in Africa by the European powers was in the view of the BBC Trust regarded as exploitation which had no redeeming features, and this was regarded as a proposition which was simply not open to argument.

A significant indication of the depth of ignorance underlying this investigation was the reference to an unspecified source from St. John's College, Cambridge. The source is quoted as authority for the proposition that 'by 1914 [the assumed end of the *period of the Scramble for Africa] there were only two truly independent states remaining –Liberia and Ethiopia.'* The use of the word 'remaining' was clearly intended to indicate that the Scramble for Africa involved the takeover by conquest or other form of acquisition of independent states, which is an outrageous falsification of history. The Scramble for Africa involved the drawing of lines on the map and the creation of new colonial entities, in many cases by the making of treaties between representatives of the European powers and African chiefs. Some African chiefs such as the emirs of Northern Nigeria were powerful and held sway over substantial territory and populations, others exercised a much more modest rule and in some parts such as Eastern Nigeria, there were no identifiable chiefs at all. The concept of an independent state, a status attained by recognition by other states, was well understood in the nineteenth century and in no cases were the chiefs heads of such independent states. Leaving aside the Arab States north of the Africa, in contact with Europe since antiquity, **Liberia and Ethiopia were the only independent states so understood in the continent before as well as after the Scramble for Africa.** The European powers created newly defined territories whose boundaries in due course became the frontiers of newly independent states in the latter half of the twentieth century, frontiers which remain largely unchanged to this day. My response on this subject to the BBC Trust was ignored and the response which I eventually received, declaring my complaint not upheld, showed no greater understanding of colonial history than that shown by the BBC's Complaints Director.

Summary

The BBC's response to my complaint relied on a narrow and pedantic interpretation of the precise words used in the programme which were the subject of my complaint. The argument used in

Stage 1 was that the words used were meant to refer only to the years following the Scramble for Africa, understood as meaning up to 1914 and no later. The actual words used do not lend themselves to that restricted meaning. Most viewers watching the programme would be unlikely to have any close acquaintance with the detail of nineteenth-and twentieth-century African history. I obviously, because of my own colonial background, have a closer familiarity with the subject than most viewers would have and I certainly did not understand the words used in the narrow sense pleaded in defence by the BBC, nor do I so accept them now. As for the statement that colonisation created '*a system of exploitation that was every bit as shameful as the slave trade*', even the BBC eventually and with evident reluctance conceded that this was 'debateable' – to quote the word as misspelt. This is an absurd understatement; the allegation in the words quoted is an outrageous and scurrilous untruth.

As regards Stage 2, I maintain that although the reference to Zambia is specific, it was apparent to me at the time and remains obvious that following the highly disparaging and unbalanced references to the evils of colonial rule which preceded it, this was meant to convey to the viewer the clear notion that Africans generally, and not only Zambians, were glad to be rid of the colonial yoke. I pointed out that the post-independence history of Zambia, though less turbulent than that of many other African countries, has been far from happy, thus further giving the lie to the impression of blissful contentment among the people of Zambia since independence, which the words were obviously intended to convey.

Postscript

My correspondence with the BBC and the BBC Trust was mainly in early 2013 and I drew attention to the scenes of genuine jubilation which greeted the French army on their recent arrival in the towns of northern Mali after they had driven out the Islamic terrorists who had seized control of the country. At the time of writing (August 2014) when the atrocities committed by the Islamic State in northern Iraq are dominating the news, it appears that there is renewed activity on the part of Islamic militants in Mali and that they are again facing opposition from units of the French army, 15,000 of whose soldiers are still based in the country. In that correspondence I drew attention also to the following passage from the current article on Sierra Leone in Wikipedia in the paragraphs dealing with the murderous civil war in the country at the end of the 1990s and the intervention by the British Army at the beginning of this century:

> 'The situation in the country deteriorated to such an extent that British troops were deployed in operation Palliser, originally to evacuate foreign nationals. However, the British exceeded their original mandate and took full military action to finally defeat the rebels and restore order. The British were the catalysts for the ceasefire that ended the civil war. **Elements of the British Army, together with administrators and politicians, remain in Sierra Leone to this day** [Emphasis supplied], helping train the armed forces, improve the infrastructure of the country and administer financial and material aid. Tony Blair, the Prime Minister of Britain at the time of the British intervention, is regarded as a hero by the people of Sierra Leone, many of whom are keen for more British involvement.'

I regard it as very significant and a telling counterblast to the BBC's prevailing anti-colonialist ideology that the citizens of first Sierra Leone, and then Mali, should ecstatically welcome intervention by the armies of their former supposedly oppressive colonial masters many years after independence, to rescue them from Islamist and other forces which can truly be regarded as modern oppressors.

SPORT – NOT FOR ME

I was never enthusiastic about or showed any great aptitude for any form of sport, so it may seem a little odd to devote a chapter to the subject. But for some of the most important years of my life I was in environments where sport was an obsession and lack of talent in any sporting activity was regarded as a significant failing. I could not help being affected by this intellectual and social climate and being psychologically adversely affected by it for much of my early life.

I moved to Bolton School in 1945, just after the end of the war, at the age of 14. It was formally a public school, judged by the Headmaster's membership of the Headmasters' Conference and academically and in every other way would have been regarded at the time as superior to Darwen Grammar School, where I was a pupil from 1941 to 1945. It was well endowed by William Hesketh Lever, founder of Unilever. It had an excellent academic record as judged by results in School Certificate and Higher School Certificate examinations, then the main public examinations at ages 16 and 18, and sent many boys on to scholarships and places in leading universities, especially Cambridge. However, achievement in sports was regarded as very important, and in some ways might be regarded as even more important than academic attainment.

The school was divided artificially into Houses, on the lines of the major public schools such as Eton and Harrow, though as it was not a boarding school the Houses had no existence as separate buildings. Boys were allocated to one of four Houses – Manchester, Wigan, Chorley and Blackburn, the names of neighbouring large towns, depending on where their homes were. As I was from Darwen I was automatically made a member of Blackburn House. The Houses competed against each other in cricket, football, swimming and athletics and results of House matches were taken seriously. There was no attempt to use the House system as a means of assessing academic results or other activities such as music, drama or the debating society. However, every boy was assigned to a Housemaster, whose task it was to keep a record of how active the boy was in non-academic fields. My own housemaster was a mathematics teacher who would go through my progress once a term, but who did not teach the class of which I was a member and with whom otherwise I never had any contact.

I never had any great interest or competence in football or cricket. On one of the few occasions I ever tried to play football I was reprimanded by my teammates for scoring an own goal. Attempts at cricket were equally rare and I would invariably be posted to field at long stop and be last man in to bat. I cherish the memory of one occasion when I went in to bat and all the fielders relaxed, taking it for granted that I would be bowled out first ball. Their complacency was immediately shattered when I managed to hit the ball and run two, so they closed in on me and I was clean bowled with the second ball. At one stage hockey was introduced as an additional sport, and I tried that but with no greater success than I had had at any other game. Wednesday afternoons were set aside for participation in games, and after my lack of any noticeable ability had been assessed I joined other members of the school's awkward squad on cross country runs. None of us showed any great competitive urge and for some of the distance the run slowed down to a chatty and sociable walk.

It was expected of every boy that he should be able to swim ten lengths non-stop and this was one of the items on every Housemaster's check list. I could swim and still do swim regularly for exercise, but I have never been a strong swimmer and certainly would never have attempted any form of competitive swimming. When I swim now I never attempt more than four lengths non-stop. I was pressed by my Housemaster to make good the deficiency in my House record and eventually made it, but it was a struggle for me. Boys who achieved this were given a certificate, which was awarded by the Headmaster in a school assembly. When I was given my certificate nearly all the other boys receiving theirs were in the first or second forms, whereas I at the end of the queue was in the fifth and this belated accomplishment aroused a great deal of good-humoured but slightly sarcastic comments from my contemporaries, which was embarrassing for me.

Bolton School, like most other secondary schools at the time, had prefects who were appointed because of their particular merits or achievements. They had their own common room, special places in assembly, and a limited role in enforcing discipline on younger boys. They even had authority to administer beatings for certain offences, something which would be unthinkable now even for teachers when corporal punishment in schools is completely banned. Prefects were chosen from captains of teams or boys who were otherwise prominent in sport and just a few who had shown some ability in other fields. I had no talent for sport, but I had an excellent academic record and ended my school career by winning an open scholarship to my college at Cambridge. I was Secretary of the School's Debating Society and active in the school's music. It was always a source of grievance for me that notwithstanding this record I was never considered suitable material for the honour of being appointed a prefect. I was not a unique case. A slightly older contemporary was Irving Wardle, later drama critic of The Times, a brilliant pianist and an outstanding actor who took the title role in a school production of Hamlet, but with no interest in sports. He also was never appointed, though whether he harboured any grievance about that I do not know.

I recall one particularly embarrassing collective experience. Boxing was a school sport, one in which I never engaged and would have found most uncongenial, to put it mildly. On one occasion there were final bouts from a boxing competition, held to determine the winners. For this the whole school was ordered to attend and watch a succession of bouts in the school's gymnasium. One would have expected this to be an occasion for showing some enthusiasm, but we were all ordered to be completely silent during the rounds. No doubt the headmaster in making this order was concerned that if the boys were allowed to show their feelings for particular fighters, it might result in some unpleasant comments being shouted and undermine the decorum which he was anxious to preserve, but in retrospect I would need to ask what was the point of insisting that the whole school should be present and maintain strict silence.

Outside school I was conscious that I lived a rather lonely life, not having much in common with other members of my family or other people with whom I came into contact. I decided that I ought to try to overcome this by going to football matches and in this I had some encouragement from my father who was a supporter of Blackburn Rovers. I tried this for a few matches but was frankly bored by the experience and could never understand the enthusiasm and passion evinced by others around me in the crowd. I could not wait for the final whistle. I eventually realised that I was wasting my time and thankfully gave up.

In the course of my time as Company Secretary of Wellcome, I was sometimes invited to attend sporting events. One such event that I vividly remember was a football match in a huge modern air-conditioned stadium in Vancouver, where I was taking part in negotiations between Wellcome and a company which was an agent of the British Columbia government. It was my first visit to that beautiful city, it was summer time and I would have loved to have a free evening to take advantage of my surroundings, but obviously could not refuse the invitation to go to the match and be entertained in a VIP box. I was thankful that we were not expected to stay after half-time. On another

214

occasion I was invited by the company's insurance brokers to go to the Oxford v Cambridge rugby match at Twickenham, watching from the comfort of a VIP box with champagne lunch provided. I have never watched rugby in my life and would have had no understanding at all of what was happening on the pitch, so I politely declined the offer, causing some consternation to my putative hosts.

Cambridge and Rowing

At Cambridge I was still affected by the psychological climate which created the pressure to have some sort of sporting achievement to one's credit, though the pressure was in no way comparable to that of which I had been conscious at Bolton School. It was certainly desirable to have some sort of pleasurable pursuit as a break from attending lectures and working for the Tripos examinations, but it need not have been sport. With the benefit of hindsight it has long been obvious to me that I ought to have devoted more time and enthusiasm to music than I in fact did. But I suffered from the feeling that I was just not talented enough to compete with other Cambridge musicians. I was a reasonably good pianist and in my second year shared rooms in college with Keith Pemberton, now sadly deceased, a friend from Bolton School with whom I had started playing piano duets while at school. We hired a piano during that year and made good use of it. We might perhaps have had a certain amount of success in taking part in concerts organised by student music bodies but did not make any effort in that direction. In the college there were occasional Sunday night musical gatherings in the Master's Lodge and we played duets at two of these, but that was as far as our involvement in performances of piano music went. At school I had been a member of the choral society and could have tried to become a member of one or other of the choirs in Cambridge, but I felt that I was probably not good enough. The best of the choirs could be choosy enough to require that aspiring members undergo an audition to test their vocal and sight reading abilities, and I doubted whether I would have passed the tests. I did not even try and was probably seriously undervaluing myself.

It was a kind of inferiority complex which prevented me making a serious attempt at finding a niche for myself in Cambridge's undergraduate music and which prevented me from doing justice to my own abilities. So I languished in what I now think was surely a mistaken belief that I would be unlikely to succeed in attempting this particular route to making a mark socially in Cambridge but still needed to belong to some kind of activity other than my academic work. Field sports were out so in desperation I decided to try rowing and this was the sport which occupied much of my time for my second and third years. It meant three or sometimes four afternoons training on the river and taking part in the races at the end of each term, the Fairbairn timed race in December and the bumping races in the other two terms. Rowing had the advantage for someone like myself that the qualities of basic enthusiasm and aptitude for skilled hand and eye coordination, which are the necessary attributes of anyone hoping to achieve even a modest degree of distinction in ball games are not needed. Rowing calls for precise coordination of movements by every member of the crew and an iron discipline which ensures that all eight blades enter and leave the water at exactly the same angle and the same time with the result that the boat moves quickly and smoothly. The oarsmen have to accept that they are simply part of a powerful engine and the only scope for individuality rests with the cox who has to steer the boat and with stroke, the oarsman immediately facing cox, who sets the pace which the other seven oarsmen have to follow.

Rowing is a physically demanding form of exercise, but there is a kind of masochistic pleasure to be derived from feeling that the boat is running smoothly once a certain level of training has been reached and the members of the crew are rowing as one. There is some excitement to be derived from the bumping races, though not so much from any timed race. I rowed in the college's second boat and admit to enjoying some of the camaraderie which training and racing entailed. I recall that in one term we had a boat club table with its own special diet at mealtimes in Hall and there would normally be a boat club dinner after end-of-term races.

Rowing was not all bad but it was not what I really wanted from life and a wholehearted pursuit of music would have been much more congenial and enjoyable. Music has been a joy and a solace to me for most of my life and I would have benefited greatly from an immersion in the rich and varied musical life of Cambridge. It might also have given me a modest amount of contact with women musicians, a welcome relief from the exclusively male environment of the law school and the boat club. There were only two women's colleges, Girton and Newnham, and even if the students at Homerton women's teacher training college and the nurses at Addenbrooke's hospital were included in the computation, the university in the early 1950s had a ratio of around eight men to one woman. This meant for most of us a quasi-monastic life during term time.

After Cambridge

Having rowed on the Cam for two years I chose to continue with this self-inflicted arduous regime by joining a crew of Devonshire Course cadets rowing under London School of Economics colours in the Head of the River Race on the Thames in the spring of 1954. But otherwise I no longer felt under any sort of compulsion to join in any particular sport unless it suited my pleasure. I reflect sadly that during the vital years from age 14 to age 23 I was constantly prey to an inferiority complex about my innate lack of enthusiasm for or competence in any form of team sport. There was no reason for me to have such a complex, but I was influenced by the anti-intellectual climate which so dominated schools and to a lesser extent universities during those years.

I began to play tennis when I was 17 and continued to play on and off until I was around 60, but only ever for pleasure and exercise, never out of any competitive zeal. I spent part of my national service in Berlin and once or twice took advantage of being able to have a game on the courts at Berlin's Olympic Stadium where the 1936 Games had taken place under Hitler, and which was in the British Sector of the city. I played occasionally on the college's courts at Cambridge and sometimes had access to a court in Sierra Leone. In India, my wife and I lived in a residential compound outside Bombay which had two courts. After we returned from India we lived for twenty-eight years in Molesey, Surrey, just over a mile from Hampton Court Palace, which provided a set of public tennis courts. For some years I played there on Sunday mornings with our old friend, the late John Edwards as my opponent. He was always a better player than I was, so he won most of the matches. Latterly, I found that I never won at all, and this became a little depressing. Losing most matches was tolerable, but when I was no longer able to win at all I decided it was time to give up, which I did. Since then I have never attempted tennis or any other game. I am happy to watch the Oxford and Cambridge boat race on television and also some of the matches at Wimbledon, but am otherwise happy to leave sport in all its forms to the rest of the world.

POSTSCRIPT – REFLECTIONS ON THE EU REFERENDUM RESULT

Written immediately after the EU referendum on 23 June 2016

This is a subject I had not intended to cover in this book. I have always been pro EU and after all the turmoil and anguish on both sides of the debate in the past four months I was expecting with a degree of modest confidence that the result of the referendum would be for Remain. I was in part basing this on the historical fact that British experience of referendums has up to now been wholly that of a popular vote in view of maintaining the status quo. This was the case with the votes on EEC membership in 1975, the Alternative Vote referendum in 2009 and the Scottish Independence referendum in 2014. As the Vote Leave campaign was unable to talk in more than bold and general terms about what the government's programme for agreements to replace the EU treaties would be if the campaign were to be successful, it was not unreasonable to assume on the basis of this past experience that the majority, perhaps only a small majority, would vote to remain. That did not happen, and I do not propose to add to the torrent of millions of often acrimonious words that have been poured out by both campaigns and which continue to dominate the airwaves and print media. I feel greatly saddened by the result of the referendum, but I just want to consider the EU and related topics from a personal point of view, in keeping with the content of the rest of this book.

I have explained at various points in this book that I was "good at languages" to use a once common expression and had firsts in French and German in the Modern Languages Tripos Part I. (It says something for the general level of national linguistic incompetence that for a native English speaker to be able to manage to hold a modest conversation in any other language than his own is regarded almost as a mark of genius, whereas we take it for granted that well educated Dutch, Germans, Swedes and almost any other nationality can speak fluent and idiomatic English as almost an incidental supplement to their attainments in medicine, engineering or whatever.) So I naturally thought of the Foreign Service as my first choice of career, only to be sadly disappointed in that endeavour.

While in Sierra Leone, a country having a border with what was then French Guinea I had occasional opportunities to meet French expatriates or French speaking Africans and talk with them in their own language. Chances to speak any language other than English or Hindi in my later years in India were rare and for the most part I contented myself with a subscription to the French weekly '*Le Figaro Hébdomadaire*' by air mail. In the chapter '*Dagenham and Bombay*' I mentioned my return with family after resigning from being Company Secretary of an Indian company. We left Bombay by P&O liner on 1 January 1964 and on the ship I made good use of my portable typewriter producing job applications. In the latter part of 1963 Britain's first application to join the EEC was being considered by the original Member States and the possibility of Britain's accession and thus creating new opportunities for British linguists was for me an exciting prospect, part of my motivation for leaving India. But it was while we were at sea that we had the news that General de Gaulle, President of France, had shocked the world by vetoing Britain's application. I felt this almost as a personal blow.

In an earlier chapter I described my involvement with the European airbus project as legal adviser to Hawker Siddeley Aviation, the most exciting time of my working life. This was in 1968-1969, before Britain's accession on 1 January 1973. The airbus has been a great European success story, combining the aircraft industries of France, Britain, Germany and Spain and rivalling Boeing to produce and sell planes to the world's major airlines. While working with Hawker Siddeley I also took part in negotiating substantial sales contracts for civil aircraft for a French regional airline in Brittany, the Belgian air force and the German *Bundesanstalt für Flugsicherung* (Federal flight safety organisation). The latter was a huge contract worth many millions, written and negotiated in German. I was the only member of our team who knew German, so I was effectively in charge. These contracts had no connection with the EEC but I found my involvement in them exciting at a time when British accession was imminent.

Soon after accession in 1973, while still employed by Hawker Siddeley Aviation, I applied for a job with the European Commission, which was advertising vacancies for lawyers and recruiting in Britain. I found the thought of moving to Brussels and working in that cosmopolitan environment very appealing. I was interviewed twice in London, once by the head of the Commission's legal service and once by a large panel of officials of different nationalities. On the latter occasion I was able to acquit myself well answering in English, French and German questions directed at assessing the state of my knowledge of the EEC's affairs. Sadly I was never positively offered a job with the Commission, but neither was I told that my application had failed. Another disappointment.

During my time with Wellcome I paid many enjoyable visits to European cities on the company's business, including visits with the entire board to Hamburg, Rome, Madrid and Nice. Wellcome had well established subsidiaries in France, Germany, Spain and Italy. In negotiation we had to have regard always to the provisions of relevant EEC laws, and always had to take particular care to ensure that we did not fall foul of the EEC's equivalent of the American anti-trust laws.

I have long been an armchair railway enthusiast as well as being pro-European. I therefore simply had to apply for shares in Eurotunnel when it was promoted, even though I realised at the time that it was most unlikely ever to be a profitable investment. I bought 750 shares for £3500. In the last few years Eurotunnel has been able to pay out minute dividends, but the only cash returns I have had total less than five pounds. I did however have the benefit of free passages on Le Shuttle once a year for ten years ending in 2004. The company found that it needed capital to complete the construction of the tunnel far exceeding what it had been able to raise from shareholders and had to borrow huge sums from over 200 banks. The company later was faced with the impossibility of paying off its huge debts and in order to remain solvent had to restructure its capital base by issuing new shares in lieu of cash. This dilution meant that I had to surrender 750 original shares in exchange for 18 new ones.

Eurosceptic contemporaries sometimes lament what they regard as a failure by Britain to exploit fully its position at the centre of the Commonwealth and I have known some who regard it as an act of betrayal for Britain to join the EEC and, as they see it, abandon the Commonwealth. My impression is that by 'the Commonwealth' these Eurosceptics mean only what used to be called the white Dominions, Canada, Australia and New Zealand and their limited definition does not include for example, India, Pakistan and Nigeria. It must surely be obvious now that these historic links, while they may have some political or even sentimental significance, are of much reduced economic importance. The main economic ties of Australia are now with China and those of Canada are and always have been with the USA.

My own early history indicates strong involvement with the Commonwealth, spending years in Sierra Leone and India. While I was Company Secretary of Wellcome I was a director of subsidiaries in India, Pakistan and Nigeria and had occasion to visit Singapore and Hong Kong on the company's business. I have a daughter who married a Canadian Army officer and has two children who have dual British and Canadian nationality. I do not see that my enthusiasm for Europe is in any way incompatible with this personal history. I am greatly saddened that such enthusiasm should now be regarded as almost unpatriotic.

I have devoted a whole chapter of this book to my personal campaign to defend Britain's imperial record, a subject on which I still feel passionate. My concern is to protect our history against unjustified and often malevolent disparagement. But it is history. I cannot sympathise with, still less share, sentiments which are decidedly anti-European and evince a hankering after Britain's imperial past which I do not share. I have observed this frame of mind among middle class men of my own generation and which to some extent are based on unspoken assumptions of racial superiority vis à vis the citizens of other European nations. This makes it all the more ironic that those people who cherish such sentiments at the same time complain about the EU as if Brussels was the seat of a mighty empire and Britain a mere vassal colony with no say in its own destiny.